W9-AEP-302

POETRY

from

Literature for Our Time

POETRY

from

Literature for Our Time

THIRD EDITION

Edited by

HARLOW O. WAITE

BENJAMIN P. ATKINSON

Granger Index Reprint Series

BOOKS FOR LIBRARIES PRESS
FREEPORT, NEW YORK

STANDARD BOOK NUMBER:
8369-6117-X

LIBRARY OF CONGRESS CATALOG CARD NUMBER:
72-108589

MANUFACTURED
BY
HALLMARK LITHOGRAPHERS, INC.
IN THE U.S.A.

INTRODUCTION

Wɪᴛʜ the publication of the Third Edition of *Literature for Our Time*, we have again found that a number of teachers are particularly interested in the revised collection of poems which comprise Part V of the book. We are therefore issuing that collection of poetry as a separate volume.

In this new edition we have dropped numerous poems which proved to have limited, or too topical, appeal; we have added to the poems of Frost, Eliot, Auden, and Thomas; we have added a selection of the work of seven poets who have come to notice since 1950. The added Frost poems should make possible a more thorough study of his work, even as the addition of Auden's "Nones" to his already included "Prime" will suggest the range and depth of the sequence of which they are a part. Eliot's "East Coker" and four more Thomas poems provide more adequate representation of their work. The selections we have made from several "new" poets will suggest the variety of subject matter, the freedom as well as the restrictions of style and form, the enthusiasm and the restraint which are in the worlds of these poets. As we have noted in our Prefatory Note, they augur well for the future of poetry.

In reprinting the poetry section as it stands in this Third Edition, we have been aware that some teachers might regret the exclusion of the seven poems which appear elsewhere in the original volume, six of them in Part I and one in Part VI. We have accordingly included these seven poems at the end of this introduction. They are arranged here to help the student to cultivate some of the skills necessary to reading poems. But if they are read in any order or just for themselves, they will also acquaint him with some of the major themes which have preoccupied the poets of the past hundred years. As a group they thus serve to introduce this collection of poetry.

Cummings' "in Just-spring," for example, presents an experience that is familiar to most readers and presents it simply, directly, and without apparent comment. At the same time, the form of the poem is unfamiliar to many readers because the poet is using certain devices to make more immediate the experience itself. Thus, he uses the capital "J" to indicate that the poem is of the precise moment when we are sure that spring has actually arrived. Again, he spaces words and lines to suggest the distance of the balloonman's whistle and the running together of the children.

The four poems that follow are more concerned with the interpretation of experience through evaluation and consequent advice. MacLeish in "Eleven" preserves the experience itself and metaphorically suggests what it may lead to, while Yeats, Sandburg, and Fearing speak directly out of their own experience in an attempt to give form and order to what they value. Finally we turn back nearly a hundred years to read how Arnold and Whitman stated the issue of doubt and faith that each of us must face. In generalizing terms that are no less an immediate experience than the simple descriptions of Cummings' spring, these older poets express what remains a dominant concern of our time and of all time—the future.

A brief discussion of the poems in Part V, in the form of a Prefatory Note, precedes the poems themselves.

Syracuse University   H. O. W.
Hobart and William Smith Colleges   B. P. A.
March 1, 1958

CONTENTS

Contents

Contents

Contents

Contents

IN JUST-SPRING

by E. E. CUMMINGS

in Just-
spring   when the world is mud-
luscious the little
lame balloonman

whistles   far   and wee

and eddieandbill come
running from marbles and
piracies and it's
spring

when the world is puddle-wonderful

the queer
old balloonman whistles
far   and   wee
and bettyandisabel come dancing

from hop-scotch and jump-rope and

it's
spring
and
          the

                    goat-footed

balloonman   whistles
far
and
wee

ELEVEN

by ARCHIBALD MACLEISH

And summer mornings the mute child, rebellious,
Stupid, hating the words, the meanings, hating
The Think now, Think, the O but Think! would leave
On tiptoe the three chairs on the verandah
And crossing tree by tree the empty lawn
Push back the shed door and upon the sill
Stand pressing out the sunlight from his eyes
And enter and with outstretched fingers feel
The grindstone and behind it the bare wall
And turn and in the corner on the cool
Hard earth sit listening. And one by one,
Out of the dazzled shadow in the room
The shapes would gather, the brown plowshare, spades,
Mattocks, the polished helves of picks, a scythe
Hung from the rafters, shovels, slender tines
Glinting across the curve of sickles—shapes
Older than men were, the wise tools, the iron
Friendly with earth. And sit there quiet, breathing
The harsh dry smell of withered bulbs, the faint
Odor of dung, the silence. And outside
Beyond the half-shut door the blind leaves
And the corn moving. And at noon would come,
Up from the garden, his hard crooked hands
Gentle with earth, his knees still earth-stained, smelling
Of sun, of summer, the old gardener, like
A priest, like an interpreter, and bend
Over his baskets.

        And they would not speak:
They would say nothing. And the child would sit there
Happy as though he had no name, as though
He had been no one: like a leaf, a stem,
Like a root growing—

The selection from Archibald MacLeish *Poems 1924-1933* is used by permission of the publishers, Houghton Mifflin Company.

A PRAYER FOR MY DAUGHTER

by William Butler Yeats

Once more the storm is howling, and half
hid
Under this cradle-hood and coverlid
My child sleeps on. There is no obstacle
But Gregory's wood and one bare hill
Whereby the haystack- and roof-leveling
wind,
Bred on the Atlantic, can be stayed;
And for an hour I have walked and prayed
Because of the great gloom that is in my
mind.

I have walked and prayed for this young
child an hour
And heard the sea-wind scream upon the
tower,
And under the arches of the bridge, and
scream
In the elms above the flooded stream;
Imagining in excited reverie
That the future years had come,
Dancing to a frenzied drum,
Out of the murderous innocence of the
sea.

May she be granted beauty, and yet not
Beauty to make a stranger's eye distraught,
Or hers before a looking-glass, for such,
Being made beautiful overmuch,
Consider beauty a sufficient end,
Lose natural kindness and maybe
The heart-revealing intimacy
That chooses right, and never find a friend.

Helen being chosen found life flat and dull
And later had much trouble from a fool,
While that great Queen, that rose out of
the spray,
Being fatherless could have her way

Yet chose a bandy-leggèd smith for man.
It's certain that fine women eat
A crazy salad with their meat
Whereby the Horn of Plenty is undone.

In courtesy I'd have her chiefly learned;
Hearts are not had as a gift but hearts are
earned
By those that are not entirely beautiful;
Yet many, that have played the fool
For beauty's very self, has charm made
wise,
And many a poor man that has roved,
Loved and thought himself beloved,
From a glad kindness cannot take his eyes.

May she become a flourishing hidden tree
That all her thoughts may like the linnet
be,
And have no business but dispensing
round
Their magnanimities of sound,
Nor but in merriment begin a chase,
Nor but in merriment a quarrel.
Oh, may she live like some green laurel
Rooted in one dear perpetual place.

My mind, because the minds that I have
loved,
The sort of beauty that I have approved,
Prosper but little, has dried up of late,
Yet knows that to be choked with hate
May well be of all evil chances chief.
If there's no hatred in a mind
Assault and battery of the wind
Can never tear the linnet from the leaf.

An intellectual hatred is the worst,
So let her think opinions are accursed.

From W. B. Yeats, *Collected Poems*. By permission of The Macmillan Company, publishers.

Have I not seen the loveliest woman born
Out of the mouth of Plenty's horn,
Because of her opinionated mind
Barter that horn and every good
By quiet natures understood
For an old bellows full of angry wind?

Considering that, all hatred driven hence,
The soul recovers radical innocence
And learns at last that it is self-delighting,
Self-appeasing, self-affrighting,
And that its own sweet will is Heaven's
    will;

She can, though every face should scowl
And every windy quarter howl
Or every bellows burst, be happy still.

And may her bridegroom bring her to a
    house
Where all's accustomed, ceremonious;
For arrogance and hatred are the wares
Peddled in the thoroughfares.
How but in custom and in ceremony
Are innocence and beauty born?
Ceremony's a name for the rich horn,
And custom for the spreading laurel tree

from THE PEOPLE, YES

by CARL SANDBURG

9

A father sees a son nearing manhood.
What shall he tell that son?
"Life is hard; be steel; be a rock."
And this might stand him for the storms
and serve him for humdrum and monotony
and guide him amid sudden betrayals
and tighten him for slack moments.
"Life is a soft loam; be gentle; go easy."
And this too might serve him.
Brutes have been gentled where lashes failed.
The growth of a frail flower in a path up
has sometimes shattered and split a rock.
A tough will counts. So does desire.
So does a rich soft wanting.
Without rich wanting nothing arrives.
Tell him too much money has killed men
and left them dead years before burial:
the quest of lucre beyond a few easy needs
has twisted good enough men
sometimes into dry thwarted worms.
Tell him time as a stuff can be wasted.

From *The People, Yes* by Carl Sandburg. Copyright, 1936, by Harcourt, Brace and Company, Inc.

Tell him to be a fool every so often
and to have no shame over having been a fool
yet learning something out of every folly
hoping to repeat none of the cheap follies
thus arriving at intimate understanding
of a world numbering many fools.
Tell him to be alone often and get at himself
and above all tell himself no lies about himself
whatever the white lies and protective fronts
he may use amongst other people.
Tell him solitude is creative if he is strong
and the final decisions are made in silent rooms.
Tell him to be different from other people
if it comes natural and easy being different.
Let him have lazy days seeking his deeper motives.
Let him seek deep for where he is a born natural.
Then he may understand Shakespeare
and the Wright brothers, Pasteur, Pavlov,
Michael Faraday and free imaginations
bringing changes into a world resenting change.
He will be lonely enough
to have time for the work
he knows as his own.

ANY MAN'S ADVICE TO HIS SON

by KENNETH FEARING

If you have lost the radio beam, then guide yourself by the sun or the stars.
(By the North Star at night, and in daytime by the compass and the sun.)
Should the sky be overcast and there are neither stars nor a sun, then steer by dead reckoning.
If the wind and direction and speed are not known, then trust to your wits and your luck.

Do you follow me? Do you understand? Or is this too difficult to learn?
But you must and you will, it is important that you do,
Because there may be troubles even greater than these that I have said.

Because, remember this: Trust no man fully.
Remember: If you must shoot at another man squeeze, do not jerk the trigger.
Otherwise you may miss and die, yourself, at the hand of some other man's son.

From Kenneth Fearing, *Collected Poems*. Copyright, 1940, by Random House, Inc. Reprinted by permission of Random House, Inc. Originally appeared in *The New Yorker*.

And remember: In all this world there is nothing so easily squandered, or once gone,
so completely lost as life.

I tell you this because I remember you when you were small,
And because I remember all your monstrous infant boasts and lies,
And the way you smiled, and how you ran and climbed, as no one else quite did,
and how you fell and were bruised,
And because there is no other person, anywhere on earth, who remembers these
things as clearly as I do now.

DOVER BEACH

by MATTHEW ARNOLD

The sea is calm to-night,
The tide is full, the moon lies fair
Upon the straits;—on the French coast the
light
Gleams and is gone; the cliffs of England
stand,
Glimmering and vast, out in the tranquil
bay.
Come to the window, sweet is the night-
air!
Only, from the long line of spray
Where the sea meets the moon-blanched
land.
Listen! you hear the grating roar
Of pebbles which the waves draw back,
and fling,
At their return, up the high strand,
Begin, and cease, and then again begin,
With tremulous cadence slow, and bring
The eternal note of sadness in.

Sophocles long ago
Heard it on the Aegaean, and it brought
Into his mind the turbid ebb and flow

Of human misery; we
Find also in the sound a thought,
Hearing it by this distant northern sea.

The Sea of Faith
Was once, too, at the full, and round
earth's shore
Lay like the folds of a bright girdle furled.
But now I only hear
Its melancholy, long, withdrawing roar,
Retreating, to the breath
Of the night-wind, down the vast edges
drear
And naked shingles of the world.
Ah, love, let us be true
To one another! for the world, which
seems
To lie before us like a land of dreams,
So various, so beautiful, so new,
Hath really neither joy, nor love, nor light,
Nor certitude, nor peace, nor help for pain;
And we are here as on a darkling plain
Swept with confused alarms of struggle
and flight,
Where ignorant armies clash by night.

YEARS OF THE MODERN

by WALT WHITMAN

Years of the modern! years of the unperform'd!
Your horizon rises, I see it parting away for more august dramas,
I see not America only, not only Liberty's nation but other nations preparing,
I see tremendous entrances and exits, new combinations, the solidarity of races,
I see that force advancing with irresistible power on the world's stage,
(Have the old forces, the old wars, played their parts? are the acts suitable to them
    closed?)
I see Freedom, completely arm'd and victorious and very haughty, with Law on
    one side and Peace on the other,
A stupendous trio all issuing forth against the idea of caste;
What historic denouements are these we so rapidly approach?
I see men marching and countermarching by swift millions,
I see the frontiers and boundaries of the old aristocracies broken,
I see the landmarks of European kings removed,
I see this day the People beginning their landmarks, (all others give way);
Never were such sharp questions ask'd as this day,
Never was average man, his soul, more energetic, more like a God,
Lo, how he urges and urges, leaving the masses no rest!
His daring foot is on land and sea everywhere, he colonizes the Pacific, the archi-
    pelagoes,
With the steamship, the electric telegraph, the newspaper, the wholesale engines
    of war,
With these and the world-spreading factories he interlinks all geography, all lands;
What whispers are these O lands, running ahead of you, passing under the seas?
Are all nations communing? is there going to be but one heart to the globe?
Is humanity forming en-masse? for lo, tyrants tremble, crowns grow dim,
The earth, restive, confronts a new era, perhaps a general divine war,
No one knows what will happen next, such portents fill the days and nights;
Years prophetical! the space ahead as I walk, as I vainly try to pierce it, is full of
    phantoms,
Unborn deeds, things soon to be, project their shapes around me,
This incredible rush and heat, this strange ecstatic fever of dreams O years!
Your dreams O years, how they penetrate through me! (I know not whether I
    sleep or wake;)
The perform'd America and Europe grow dim, retiring in shadow behind me,
The unperform'd, more gigantic than ever, advance, advance, upon me.

From *Leaves of Grass* by Walt Whitman. With permission from Doubleday and Company, Inc.

PART V · POETRY

THE CONTEMPORARY POET writes against, and draws from, a large background of American, British, and Continental literature. Because that British background is usually studied in a Survey course, and because the Continental (particularly the French) could not be adequately represented in this volume, we have chosen to introduce this section with selections from the work of three nineteenth-century American poets. The different patterns of thought and technique found in Emerson, Dickinson, and Whitman have done their share in shaping the contemporary poet and his poem.

Thomas Hardy and A. E. Housman are frequently considered the first of the "modern" poets. Certainly the ruggedness of Hardy's poems and the precision of Housman's did much to rescue poetry from the sentimentality and false rhetoric so frequently found in the early part of this century.

The twelve poets who continue this part of the anthology range in technique from the "traditional" structures of Robinson and Frost through the symbolist patterns of Eliot to the typographical tricks of Cummings. They deal with a large and diverse subject matter: such precise things as an express train, a peach tree, a shooting gallery, and such general problems as the meaning of history, the individual's role in a world society, and the search for truth. The attitudes of the poets are also diverse: Whitman's determined optimism, Frost's search for a "Vantage Point," Eliot's early despair, Jeffers' rejection of man and society, Auden's insistence that "we must love one another or die," and Thomas' "true joy" that "sang burning in the sun."

We conclude this part of the book with a selection, necessarily limited, of the poets who have been publishing their work since 1950. These seven "new" poets deal with the old and with the new in old and new techniques. They are skillful, imaginative, moving. They are "influenced," and they are original. We have chosen these particular poems not only because they speak so poetically of our present world but also because they augur so well the future of poetry in our time.

The work of nine of the poets is preceded by excerpts from their own prose statements on the nature of poetry, the poetic process, or their attitudes toward the world. These comments can be most helpful to the reader in fully understanding the intentions of the individual poets. In the Appendix will be found a list of poems recorded by the poets. As we hear the poet read his own work, our understanding of the poem and our pleasure in it are almost always increased.

We have included only one commentary on a poem. The Kimon Friar analysis of Yeats' "Byzantium" is a clear explication of a difficult poem. The interested student will find many similar analyses of poems in the critical literature of recent years. We have provided no other commentaries or questions on the poems, believing that they should be left to the individual reader. We like to think of Robert Frost's reply to the question, "I understand the poem all right, but won't you tell me what it *means?*" He said, "If I had wanted you to know, I would have told you in the poem."

Lake Through the Locusts

Luigi Lucioni

Ode

THE RHODORA:

by RALPH WALDO EMERSON

In May, when sea-winds pierced our soli-
tudes,
I found the fresh Rhodora in the woods,
Spreading its leafless blooms in a damp
nook,
To please the desert and the sluggish
brook.
The purple petals, fallen in the pool,
Made the black water with their beauty
gay;
Here might the red-bird come his plumes
to cool,
And court the flower that cheapens his
array.
Rhodora! if the sages ask thee why
This charm is wasted on the earth and sky,
Tell them, dear, that if eyes were made for
seeing,
Then Beauty is its own excuse for being:
Why thou wert there, O rival of the rose!
I never thought to ask, I never knew:
But, in my simple ignorance, suppose
The self-same Power that brought me
there brought you.

ODE

INSCRIBED TO W. H. CHANNING

by RALPH WALDO EMERSON

Though loath to grieve
The evil time's sole patriot,
I cannot leave
My honied thought
For the priest's cant,
Or statesman's rant.

If I refuse
My study for their politique,
Which at the best is trick,
The angry Muse
Puts confusion in my brain.

But who is he that prates
Of the culture of mankind,
Of better arts and life?
Go, blindworm, go,
Behold the famous States

Harrying Mexico
With rifle and with knife!

Or who, with accent bolder,
Dare praise the freedom-loving mountain-
eer?
I found by thee, O rushing Contoocook!
And in thy valleys, Agiochook!
The jackals of the negro-holder.

The God who made New Hampshire
Taunted the lofty land
With little men;—
Small bat and wren
House in the oak:—
If earth-fire cleave
The upheaved land, and bury the folk,
The southern crocodile would grieve.

[631]

Virtue palters; Right is hence;
Freedom praised, but hid;
Funeral eloquence
Rattles the coffin-lid.

What boots thy zeal,
O glowing friend,
That would indignant rend
The northland from the south?
Wherefore? To what good end?
Boston Bay and Bunker Hill
Would serve things still;—
Things are of the snake.
The horseman serves the horse,
The neatherd serves the neat,
The merchant serves the purse,
The eater serves his meat;
'Tis the day of the chattel,
Web to weave, and corn to grind;
Things are in the saddle,
And ride mankind.

There are two laws discrete,
Not reconciled,—
Law for man, and law for thing;
The last builds town and fleet,
But it runs wild,
And doth the man unking.
'Tis fit the forest fall,
The steep be graded,
The mountain tunnelled,
The sand shaded,
The orchard planted,
The glebe tilled,
The prairie granted,
The steamer built.

Let man serve law for man;
Live for friendship, live for love,
For truth's and harmony's behoof;
The state may follow how it can,
As Olympus follows Jove.

Yet do not I implore
The wrinkled shopman to my sounding
  woods,
Nor bid the unwilling senator
Ask votes of thrushes in the solitudes.
Every one to his chosen work;—
Foolish hands may mix and mar;
Wise and sure the issues are.
Round they roll till dark is light,
Sex to sex, and even to odd;—
The over-god
Who marries Right to Might,
Who peoples, unpeoples,—
He who exterminates
Races by stronger races,
Black by white faces,—
Knows to bring honey
Out of the lion;
Grafts gentlest scion
On pirate and Turk.

The Cossack eats Poland,
Like stolen fruit;
Her last noble is ruined,
Her last poet mute:
Straight, into double band
The victors divide;
Half for freedom strike and stand;—
The astonished Muse finds thousands at
  her side.

GIVE ALL TO LOVE
by Ralph Waldo Emerson

Give all to love;
Obey thy heart;
Friends, kindred, days,
Estate, good-fame,
Plans, credit and the Muse,—
Nothing refuse.

'T is a brave master;
Let it have scope:
Follow it utterly,
Hope beyond hope:
High and more high
It dives into noon,
With wing unspent,
Untold intent;
But it is a god,
Knows its own path
And the outlets of the sky.

It was never for the mean;
It requireth courage stout.
Souls above doubt,
Valor unbending,
It will reward,—
They shall return
More than they were,
And ever ascending.

Leave all for love;
Yet, hear me, yet,
One word more thy heart behoved,
One pulse more of firm endeavor,—
Keep thee to-day,
To-morrow, forever,
Free as an Arab
Of thy beloved.

Cling with life to the maid;
But when the surprise,
First vague shadow of surmise
Flits across her bosom young,
Of a joy apart from thee,
Free be she, fancy-free;
Nor thou detain her vesture's hem,
Nor the palest rose she flung
From her summer diadem.

Though thou loved her as thyself,
As a self of purer clay,
Though her parting dims the day,
Stealing grace from all alive;
Heartily know,
When half-gods go,
The gods arrive.

DAYS[1]
by Ralph Waldo Emerson

Daughters of Time, the hypocritic Days,
Muffled and dumb like barefoot dervishes,
And marching single in an endless file,
Bring diadems and fagots in their hands.
To each they offer gifts after his will,
Bread, kingdoms, stars, and sky that holds
them all.

I, in my pleached garden, watched the
pomp,
Forgot my morning wishes, hastily
Took a few herbs and apples, and the Day
Turned and departed silent. I, too late,
Under her solemn fillet saw the scorn.

[1] "The days are ever divine, as to the first Aryans. They come and go like muffled and veiled figures, sent from a distant friendly party; but they say nothing, and if we so not use the gifts they bring, they carry them as silently away."

—Emerson, "Works and Days."

Poetry

BRAHMA[1]

by RALPH WALDO EMERSON

If the red slayer think he slays,
  Or if the slain think he is slain,
They know not well the subtle ways
  I keep, and pass, and turn again.

Far or forgot to me is near;
  Shadow and sunlight are the same;
The vanished gods to me appear;
  And one to me are shame and fame.

They reckon ill who leave me out;
  When me they fly, I am the wings;
I am the doubter and the doubt,
  And I the hymn the Brahmin sings.

The strong gods pine for my abode,
  And pine in vain the sacred Seven;
But thou, meek lover of the good!
  Find me, and turn thy back on heaven

[1] "In all nations there are minds which incline to dwell in the conception of the fundamental Unity . . . This tendency finds its highest expression in the religious writings of the East, and chiefly in the Indian Scriptures."
                                        —Emerson, essay on Plato.

Brahma is the soul or essence of all creation. The strong gods are Indra, Agni, and Yama. Emerson, aware of the difficulty of the poem, suggested, "Say Jehovah instead of Brahma," and approved the interpretation by a girl of Concord: "It simply means God everywhere."

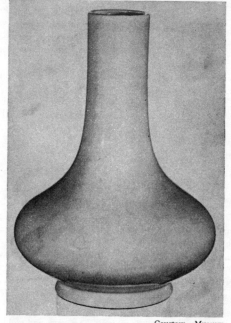

Courtesy, Museum
of Fine Arts, Boston

Chinese vase, Ch'ien-lung period.

Much Madness

THIS IS MY LETTER
by EMILY DICKINSON

This is my letter to the world,
  That never wrote to me,—
The simple news that Nature told,
  With tender majesty.   ·

Her message is committed
  To hands I cannot see;
For love of her, sweet countrymen,
  Judge tenderly of me!

I NEVER SAW
by EMILY DICKINSON

I never saw a moor,
I never saw the sea;
Yet know I how the heather looks,
And what a wave must be.

I never spoke with God,
Nor visited in heaven;
Yet certain am I of the spot
As if the chart were given.

ELYSIUM IS AS FAR
by EMILY DICKINSON

Elysium is as far as to
The very nearest room,
If in that room a friend await
Felicity or doom.

What fortitude the soul contains,
That it can so endure
The accent of a coming foot,
The opening of a door!

MUCH MADNESS
by EMILY DICKINSON

Much madness is divinest sense
To a discerning eye;
Much sense the starkest madness.
'T is the majority

In this, as all, prevails.
Assent, and you are sane;
Demur,—you're straightway dangerous,
And handled with a chain.

All poems except "Although I put away" from *Poems by Emily Dickinson,* edited by Martha Dickinson Bianchi and Alfred Leete Hampson, Little, Brown and Company.

THERE'S A CERTAIN SLANT

by EMILY DICKINSON

There's a certain slant of light,
On winter afternoons,
That oppresses, like the weight
Of cathedral tunes.

Heavenly hurt it gives us;
We can find no scar,
But internal difference
Where the meanings are.

None may teach it anything,
'T is the seal, despair,—
An imperial affliction
Sent us of the air.

When it comes, the landscape listens,
Shadows hold their breath;
When it goes, 't is like the distance
On the look of death.

SUCCESS IS COUNTED

by EMILY DICKINSON

Success is counted sweetest
By those who ne'er succeed.
To comprehend a nectar
Requires sorest need.

Not one of all the purple host
Who took the flag to-day

Can tell the definition,
So clear, of victory,

As he, defeated, dying,
On whose forbidden ear
The distant strains of triumph
Break, agonized and clear.

THE SOUL SELECTS

by EMILY DICKINSON

The soul selects her own society,
Then shuts the door;
On her divine majority
Obtrude no more.

Unmoved, she notes the chariot's pausing
At her low gate;

Unmoved, an emperor is kneeling
Upon her mat.

I've known her from an ample nation
Choose one;
Then close the valves of her attention
Like stone.

TO FIGHT ALOUD

by EMILY DICKINSON

To fight aloud is very brave,
But gallanter, I know,
Who charge within the bosom,
The cavalry of woe.

Who win, and nations do not see,
Who fall, and none observe,

Whose dying eyes no country
Regards with patriot love.

We trust, in plumed procession,
For such the angels go,
Rank after rank, with even feet
And uniforms of snow.

ALTHOUGH I PUT AWAY*

by EMILY DICKINSON

Although I put away his life,
An ornament too grand
For forehead low as mine to wear,
This might have been the hand

That sowed the flowers he preferred,
Or smoothed a homely pain,
Or pushed a pebble from his path,
Or played his chosen tune

On lute the least, the latest,
But just his ear could know
That whatsoe'er delighted it
I never would let go.

The foot to bear his errand
A little boot I know
Would leap abroad like antelope
With just the grant to do.

His weariest commandment
A sweeter to obey
Than "Hide and Seek," or skip to flutes,
Or all day chase the bee.

Your servant, Sir, will weary,
The surgeon will not come,
The world will have its own to do,
The dust will vex your fame.

The cold will force your tightest door
Some February day,
But say my apron bring the sticks
To make your cottage gay,

That I may take that promise
To Paradise with me—
To teach the angels avarice
Your kiss first taught to me!

* Copyright 1929 by Martha Dickinson Bianchi.

MY LIFE CLOSED TWICE

by EMILY DICKINSON

My life closed twice before its close;
It yet remains to see
If Immortality unveil
A third event to me,

So huge, so hopeless to conceive,
As these that twice befell.
Parting is all we know of heaven,
And all we need of hell.

JUST LOST

by EMILY DICKINSON

Just lost when I was saved!
Just felt the world go by!
Just girt me for the onset with eternity,
When breath blew back,
And on the other side
I heard recede the disappointed tide!

Therefore, as one returned, I feel,
Odd secrets of the line to tell!
Some sailor, skirting foreign shores,
Some pale reporter from the awful doors
Before the seal!

Next time, to stay!
Next time, the things to see
By ear unheard,
Unscrutinized by eye.

Next time, to tarry,
While the ages steal,—
Slow tramp the centuries,
And the cycles wheel.

ONE'S-SELF I SING

by WALT WHITMAN

One's-self I sing, a simple separate person,
Yet utter the word Democratic, the word En-Masse.

Of physiology from top to toe I sing,
Not physiognomy alone nor brain alone is worthy for the Muse,
    I say the Form complete is worthier far,
The Female equally with the Male I sing.

Of Life immense in passion, pulse, and power,
Cheerful, for freest action form'd under the laws divine,
The Modern Man I sing.

from SONG OF MYSELF

by WALT WHITMAN

I

I celebrate myself, and sing myself,
And what I assume you shall assume,
For every atom belonging to me as good belongs to you.

I loafe and invite my soul,
I lean and loafe at my ease observing a spear of summer grass.

My tongue, every atom of my blood, form'd from this soil, this air,
Born here of parents born here from parents the same, and their parents the same,
I, now thirty-seven years old in perfect health begin,
Hoping to cease not till death.

Creeds and schools in abeyance,
Retiring back a while sufficed at what they are, but never forgotten,
I harbor for good or bad, I permit to speak at every hazard,
Nature without check with original energy.

.   .   .   .

3

I have heard what the talkers were talking, the talk of the beginning and the end,
But I do not talk of the beginning or the end.

There was never any more inception than there is now,
Nor any more youth or age than there is now,
And will never be any more perfection than there is now,
Nor any more heaven or hell than there is now.

Urge and urge and urge,
Always the procreant urge of the world.
Out of the dimness opposite equals advance, always substance and increase, always
    sex,
Always a knit of identity, always distinction, always a breed of life.

To elaborate is no avail, learn'd and unlearn'd feel that it is so.

Sure as the most certain sure, plumb in the uprights, well entretied, braced in the
    beams,
Stout as a horse, affectionate, haughty, electrical,
I and this mystery here we stand.

Clear and sweet is my soul, and clear and sweet is all that is not my soul.

Lack one lacks both, and the unseen is proved by the seen,
Till that becomes unseen and receives proof in its turn.

Showing the best and dividing it from the worst age vexes age,
Knowing the perfect fitness and equanimity of things, while they discuss I am silent,
    and go bathe and admire myself.
Welcome is every organ and attribute of me, and of any man hearty and clean,
Not an inch nor a particle of an inch is vile, and none shall be less familiar than
    the rest.

I am satisfied—I see, dance, laugh, sing;
As the hugging and loving bed-fellow sleeps at my side through the night, and
    withdraws at the peep of the day with stealthy tread,
Leaving me baskets cover'd with white towels swelling the house with their plenty,
Shall I postpone my acceptation and realization and scream at my eyes,
That they turn from gazing after and down the road,
And forthwith cipher and show me to a cent,
Exactly the value of one and exactly the value of two, and which is ahead? . . .

30

All truths wait in all things,
They neither hasten their own delivery nor resist it,

Song of Myself

They do not need the obstetric forceps of the surgeon,
The insignificant is as big to me as any,
(What is less or more than a touch?)

Logic and sermons never convince,
The damp of the night drives deeper into my soul.

(Only what proves itself to every man and woman is so,
Only what nobody denies is so.)

A minute and a drop of me settle my brain,
I believe the soggy clods shall become lovers and lamps,
And a compend of compends is the meat of a man or woman,
And a summit and flower there is the feeling they have for each other,
And they are to branch boundlessly out of that lesson until it becomes omnific,
And until one and all shall delight us, and we them.

.   .   .   .

52

The spotted hawk swoops by and accuses me, he complains of my gab and my
    loitering.

I too am not a bit tamed, I too am untranslatable,
I sound my barbaric yawp over the roofs of the world.

The last scud of day holds back for me,
It flings my likeness after the rest and true as any on the shadow'd wilds,
It coaxes me to the vapor and the dusk.

I depart as air, I shake my white locks at the runaway sun,
I effuse my flesh in eddies, and drift it in lacy jags.

I bequeath myself to the dirt to grow from the grass I love,
If you want me again look for me under your boot-soles.

You will hardly know who I am or what I mean,
But I shall be good health to you nevertheless,
And filter and fibre your blood.

Failing to fetch me at first keep encouraged,
Missing me one place search another,
I stop somewhere waiting for you.

WHEN LILACS LAST IN THE DOORYARD BLOOM'D

by WALT WHITMAN

1

When lilacs last in the dooryard bloom'd,
And the great star early droop'd in the western sky in the night,
I mourn'd, and yet shall mourn with ever-returning spring.

Ever-returning spring, trinity sure to me you bring,
Lilac blooming perennial and drooping star in the west,
And thought of him I love.

2

O powerful western fallen star!
O shades of night—O moody, tearful night!
O great star disappear'd—O the black murk that hides the star!
O cruel hands that hold me powerless—O helpless soul of me!
O harsh surrrounding cloud that will not free my soul.

3

In the dooryard fronting an old farm-house near the white-wash'd palings,
Stands the lilac-bush tall-growing with heart-shaped leaves of rich green,
With many a pointed blossom rising delicate, with the perfume strong I love,
With every leaf a miracle—and from this bush in the dooryard,
With delicate-color'd blossoms and heart-shaped leaves of rich green,
A sprig with its flower I break.

4

In the swamp in secluded recesses,
A shy and hidden bird is warbling a song.
Solitary the thrush,
The hermit withdrawn to himself, avoiding the settlements,
Sings by himself a song.

Song of the bleeding throat,
Death's outlet song of life, (for well dear brother I know,
If thou wast not granted to sing thou would'st surely die.)

5

Over the breast of the spring, the land, amid cities,
Amid lanes and through old woods, where lately the violets peep'd from the ground,
    spotting the gray debris,
Amid the grass in the fields each side of the lanes, passing the endless grass,
Passing the yellow-spear'd wheat, every grain from its shroud in the dark-brown
    fields uprisen,
Passing the apple-tree blows of white and pink in the orchards,
Carrying a corpse to where it shall rest in the grave,
Night and day journeys a coffin.

6

Coffin that passes through lanes and streets,
Through day and night with the great cloud darkening the land,
With the pomp of the inloop'd flags with the cities draped in black,
With the show of the States themselves as of crape-veil'd women standing,
With processions long and winding and the flambeaus of the night,
With the countless torches lit, with the silent sea of faces and the unbared heads,
With the waiting depot, the arriving coffin, and the sombre faces,
With dirges through the night, with the thousand voices rising strong and solemn,
With all the mournful voices of the dirges pour'd around the coffin,
The dim-lit churches and the shuddering organs—where amid these you journey,
With the tolling tolling bells' perpetual clang,
Here, coffin that slowly passes,
I give you my sprig of lilac.

7

(Nor for you, for one alone,
Blossoms and branches green to coffins all I bring,
For fresh as the morning, thus would I chant a song for you O sane and sacred death.

All over bouquets of roses,
O death, I cover you over with roses and early lilies,
But mostly and now the lilac that blooms the first,
Copious I break, I break the sprigs from the bushes,
With loaded arms I come, pouring for you,
For you and the coffins all of you O death.)

8

O western orb sailing the heaven,
Now I know what you must have meant as a month since I walk'd,

As I walk'd in silence the transparent shadowy night,
As I saw you had something to tell as you bent to me night after night,
As you droop'd from the sky low down as if to my side, (while the other stars all
    look'd on,)
As we wander'd together the solemn night, (for something I know not what kept
    me from sleep,)
As the night advanced, and I saw on the rim of the west how full you were of woe,
As I stood on the rising ground in the breeze in the cool transparent night,
As I watch'd where you pass'd and was lost in the netherward black of the night,
As my soul in its trouble dissatisfied sank, as where you sad orb,
Concluded, dropt in the night, and was gone.

9

Sing on there in the swamp,
O singer bashful and tender, I hear your notes, I hear your call,
I hear, I come presently, I understand you,
But a moment I linger, for the lustrous star has detain'd me,
The star my departing comrade holds and detains me.

10

O how shall I warble myself for the dead one there I loved?
And how shall I deck my song for the large sweet soul that has gone?
And what shall my perfume be for the grave of him I love?

Sea-winds blown from east and west,
Blown from the Eastern sea and blown from the Western sea, till there on the
    prairies meeting,
These and with these and the breath of my chant,
I'll perfume the grave of him I love.

11

O what shall I hang on the chamber walls?
And what shall the pictures be that I hang on the walls,
To adorn the burial-house of him I love?

Pictures of growing spring and farms and homes,
With the Fourth-month eve at sundown, and the gray smoke lucid and bright,
With floods of the yellow gold of the gorgeous, indolent, sinking sun, burning,
    expanding the air,
With the fresh sweet herbage under foot, and the pale green leaves of the trees
    prolific,

When Lilacs Last in the Dooryard Bloom'd

In the distance the flowing glaze, the breast of the river, with a wind-dapple here
   and there,
With ranging hills on the banks, with many a line against the sky, and shadows,
And the city at hand with dwellings so dense, and stacks of chimneys,
And all the scenes of life and the workshops, and the workmen homeward returning.

12

Lo, body and soul—this land,
My own Manhattan with spires, and the sparkling and hurrying tides, and the ships,
The varied and ample land, the South and the North in the light, Ohio's shores and
   flashing Missouri,
And ever the far-spreading prairies cover'd with grass and corn.

Lo, the most excellent sun so calm and haughty,
The violet and purple morn with just-felt breezes,
The gentle soft-born measureless light,
The miracle spreading bathing all, the fulfill'd noon,
   The coming eve delicious, the welcome night and the stars,
Over my cities shining all, enveloping man and land.

13

Sing on, sing on you gray-brown bird,
Sing from the swamps, the recesses, pour your chant from the bushes,
Limitless out of the dusk, out of the cedars and pines.

Sing on dearest brother, warble your reedy song,
Loud human song, with voice of uttermost woe.

O liquid and free and tender!
O wild and loose to my soul—O wondrous singer!
You only I hear—yet the star holds me, (but will soon depart,)
Yet the lilac with mastering odor holds me.

14

Now while I sat in the day and look'd forth,
In the close of the day with its light and the fields of spring, and the farmers
   preparing their crops,
In the large unconscious scenery of my land with its lakes and forests,
In the heavenly aerial beauty, (after the perturb'd winds and the storms,)
Under the arching heavens of the afternoon swift passing, and the voices of children
   and women,

[645]

The many-moving sea-tides, and I saw the ships how they sail'd,
And the summer approaching with richness, and the fields all busy with labor,
And the infinite separate houses, how they all went on, each with its meals and
    minutia of daily usages,
And the streets how their throbbings throbb'd, and the cities pent—lo, then and
    there,
Falling upon them all and among them all, enveloping me with the rest,
Appear'd the cloud, appear'd the long black trail,
And I knew death, its thought, and the sacred knowledge of death.

Then with the knowledge of death as walking one side of me,
And the thought of death close-walking the other side of me,
And I in the middle as with companions, and as holding the hands of companions
I fled forth to the hiding receiving night that talks not,
Down to the shores of the water, the path by the swamp in the dimness,
To the solemn shadowy cedars and ghostly pines so still.

And the singer so shy to the rest receiv'd me,
The gray-brown bird I know receiv'd us comrades three,
And he sang the carol of death, and a verse for him I love.

From deep secluded recesses,
From the fragrant cedars and the ghostly pines so still,
Came the carol of the bird.

And the charm of the carol rapt me,
As I held as if by their hands my comrades in the night,
And the voice of my spirit tallied the song of the bird.

Come lovely and soothing death,
Undulate round the world, serenely arriving, arriving,
In the day, in the night, to all, to each,
Sooner or later delicate death.

Prais'd be the fathomless universe,
For life and joy, and for objects and knowledge curious,
And for love, sweet love—but praise! praise! praise!
For the sure-enwinding arms of cool-enfolding death.

Dark mother always gliding near with soft feet,
Have none chanted for thee a chant of fullest welcome?

When Lilacs Last in the Dooryard Bloom'd

Then I chant it for thee, I glorify thee above all,
I bring thee a song that when thou must indeed come, come unfalteringly.

Approach strong deliveress,
When it is so, when thou hast taken them I joyously sing the dead,
Lost in the loving floating ocean of thee,
Laved in the flood of thy bliss O death.

From me to thee glad serenades,
Dances for thee I propose saluting thee, adornments and feastings for thee,
And the sights of the open landscape and the high-spread sky are fitting,
And life and the fields, and the huge and thoughtful night.

The night in silence under many a star,
The ocean shore and the husky whispering wave whose voice I know,
And the soul turning to thee O vast and well-veil'd death,
And the body gratefully nestling close to thee.

Over the tree-tops I float thee a song,
Over the rising and sinking waves, over the myriad fields and the prairies wide,
Over the dense-pack'd cities all and the teeming wharves and ways,
I float this carol with joy, with joy to thee O death.

15

To the tally of my soul,
Loud and strong kept up the gray-brown bird,
With pure deliberate notes spreading filling the night.

Loud in the pines and cedars dim,
Clear in the freshness moist and the swamp-perfume,
And I with my comrades there in the night.

While my sight that was bound in my eyes unclosed,
As to long panoramas of visions.

And I saw askant the armies,
I saw as in noiseless dreams hundreds of battle-flags,
Borne through the smoke of the battles and pierc'd with missiles I saw them,
And carried hither and yon through the smoke, and torn and bloody,
And at last but a few shreds left in the staffs, (and all in silence,)
And the staffs all splinter'd and broken.

I saw battle-corpses, myriads of them,
And the white skeletons of young men, I saw them,
I saw the debris and debris of all the slain soldiers of the war,
But I saw they were not as was thought,
They themselves were fully at rest, they suffer'd not,
The living remain'd and suffer'd, the mother suffer'd,
And the wife and the child and the musing comrade suffer'd,
And the armies that remain'd suffer'd.

16

Passing the visions, passing the night,
Passing, unloosing the hold of my comrades' hands,
Passing the song of the hermit bird and the tallying song of my soul,
Victorious song, death's outlet song, yet varying ever-altering song,
As low and wailing, yet clear the notes, rising and falling, flooding the night,
Sadly sinking and fainting, as warning and warning, and yet again bursting with joy,
Covering the earth and filling the spread of the heaven,
As that powerful psalm in the night I heard from recesses,
Passing, I leave thee lilac with heart-shaped leaves,
I leave thee there in the door-yard, blooming, returning with spring.

I cease from my song for thee,
From my gaze on thee in the west, fronting the west, communing with thee,
O comrade lustrous with silver face in the night.

Yet each to keep and all, retrievements out of the night,
The song, the wondrous chant of the gray-brown bird,
And the tallying chant, the echo arous'd in my soul,
With the lustrous and drooping star with the countenance full of woe,
With the holders holding my hand nearing the call of the bird,
Comrades mine and I in the midst, and their memory ever to keep, for the dead I
    loved so well,
For the sweetest, wisest soul of all my days and lands—and this for his dear sake,
Lilac and star and bird twined with the chant of my soul,
There in the fragrant pines and the cedars dusk and dim.

WHEN I HEARD THE LEARN'D ASTRONOMER

by WALT WHITMAN

When I heard the learn'd astronomer,
When the proofs, the figures, were ranged in columns before me,
When I was shown the charts and diagrams, to add, divide, and measure them,
When I sitting heard the astronomer where he lectured with much applause in the
    lecture-room,
How soon unaccountable I became tired and sick,
Till rising and gliding out I wander'd off by myself,
In the mystical moist night-air, and from time to time,
Look'd up in perfect silence at the stars.

"Preface" to LATE LYRICS AND EARLIER

by THOMAS HARDY

I believe that a good deal of the robustious, swaggering optimism of recent literature is at bottom cowardly and insincere . . . but my pessimism, if pessimism it be, does not involve the assumption that the world is going to the dogs. On the contrary, my practical philosophy is distinctly meliorist. What are my books but one plea against man's inhumanity to man—to woman—and to the lower animals. . . .

. . . while I am quite aware that a thinker is not expected, and, indeed, is scarcely allowed, now more than heretofore, to state all that crosses his mind concerning existence in this universe, in his attempts to explain or excuse the presence of evil and the incongruity of penalizing the irresponsible—it must be obvious to open intelligences that, without denying the beauty and faithful service of certain venerable cults, such disallowance of "obstinate questionings" and "blank misgivings" tends to a paralysed intellectual stalemate. Heine observed nearly a hundred years ago that the soul has her eternal rights; that she will not be darkened by statutes, nor lullabied by the music of bells. And what is to-day, in allusions to the present author's pages, alleged to be "pessimism" is, in truth, only such "questionings" in the exploration of reality and is the first step towards the soul's betterment, and the body's also.

If I may be forgiven for quoting my own old words, let me repeat what I printed in this relation more than twenty years ago, and wrote much earlier, in a poem entitled "In Tenebris":

"If way to the Better there be, it exacts a full look at the Worst": that is to say, by the exploration of reality, and its frank recognition stage by stage along the survey, with an eye to the best consummation possible: briefly, evolutionary meliorism. But it is called pessimism nevertheless; under which word, expressed with condemnatory emphasis, it is regarded by many as some pernicious new thing (though so old as to underlie the Gospel scheme, and even to permeate the Greek drama); and the subject is charitably left to decent silence, as if further comment were needless.

Happily there are some who feel such Levitical passing-by to be, alas, by no means a permanent dismissal of the matter; that comment on where the world stands is very much the reverse of needless in these disordered years of our prematurely afflicted century: that amendment and not madness lies that way. And looking down the future these few hold fast to the same: that whether the human and kindred animal races survive till the exhaustion or destruction of the globe, or whether these races perish and are succeeded by others before that conclusion comes, pain to all upon it, tongued or dumb, shall be kept down to a minimum by loving-kindness, operating through scientific knowledge, and actuated by the modicum of free will conjecturally possessed by organic life when the mighty necessitating forces—unconscious or other —that have the "balancings of the clouds" happen to be in equilibrium, which may or may not be often.

. . . .

Whether owing to the barbarizing of taste in the younger minds by the dark madness of the late war, the unabashed cultivation of selfishness in all classes, the plethoric growth of knowledge simultaneously with the stunting of wisdom, "a de-grading search after outrageous stimulation" (to quote Wordsworth again), or from any other cause we seem threatened with a new Dark Age. . . . In any event poetry, pure literature in general, religion —I include religion, in its essential and undogmatic sense, because poetry and religion touch each other, or rather modulate into each other; are, indeed, often but different names for the same thing—these, I say, the visible signs of mental and emotional life, must like all other things keep moving, becoming; even though at present . . . men's minds appear as above noted, to be moving backwards rather than on.

. . . .

It may indeed be a forlorn hope, a mere dream, that of an alliance between religion which must be retained unless the world is to perish, and complete rationality, which must come, unless also the world is to perish, by means of the interfusing effect of poetry—"the breath and finer spirit of all knowledge; the impassioned expression of science," as it was defined by an English poet who was quite orthodox in his ideas. But if it be true, as Comte argued, that advance is never in a straight line, but in a looped orbit, we may, in the aforesaid ominous moving backward, be doing it *pour mieux sauter,* drawing back for a spring. I repeat that I forlornly hope so. . . . But one dares not prophesy.

HAP

by Thomas Hardy

If but some vengeful god would call to me
From up the sky, and laugh: "Thou suffering thing,
Know that thy sorrow is my ecstasy,
That thy love's loss is my hate's profiting!"

Then would I bear it, clench myself, and die,
  Steeled by the sense of ire unmerited;
Half-eased in that a Powerfuller than I
  Had willed and meted me the tears I shed.

But not so. How arrives it joy lies slain,
  And why unblooms the best hope ever sown?
—Crass Casualty obstructs the sun and rain,
  And dicing Time for gladness casts a moan. . . .
These purblind Doomsters had as readily strown
  Blisses about my pilgrimage as pain.

THE IMPERCIPIENT

(AT A CATHEDRAL SERVICE)

by THOMAS HARDY

That with this bright believing band
  I have no claim to be,
That faiths by which my comrades stand
  Seem fantasies to me,
And mirage-mists their Shining Land,
  Is a strange destiny.

Why thus my soul should be consigned
  To infelicity,
Why always I must feel as blind
  To sights my brethren see,
Why joys they've found I cannot find,
  Abides a mystery.

Since heart of mine knows not that ease
  Which they know; since it be
That He who breathes All's-Well to these
  Breathes no All's-Well to me,

My lack might move their sympathies
  And Christian charity!

I am like a gazer who should mark
  An inland company
Standing upfingered with, "Hark! hark!
  The glorious distant sea!"
And feel, "Alas, 'tis but yon dark
  And wind-swept pine to me!"

Yet I would bear my shortcomings
  With meet tranquillity,
But for the charge that blessed things
  I'd liefer not have be.
O, doth a bird deprived of wings
  Go earth-bound wilfully!

Enough. As yet disquiet clings
  About us. Rest shall we.

"AH, ARE YOU DIGGING ON MY GRAVE?"

by THOMAS HARDY

"Ah, are you digging on my grave,
　My loved one?—planting rue?"
—"No: yesterday he went to wed
One of the brightest wealth has bred.
'It cannot hurt her now,' he said,
　'That I should not be true.'"

"Then who is digging on my grave?
　My nearest dearest kin?"
—"Ah, no: they sit and think, 'What use!
What good will planting flowers produce?
No tendance of her mound can loose
　Her spirits from Death's gin.'"

"But some one digs upon my grave?
　My enemy?—prodding sly?"
—"Nay: when she heard you had passed
　the Gate
That shuts on all flesh soon or late,
She thought you no more worth her hate,
　And cares not where you lie."

"Then who is digging on my grave?
　Say—since I have not guessed!"
—"O it is I, my mistress dear,
Your little dog, who still lives near,
And much I hope my movements here
　Have not disturbed your rest?"

"Ah, yes! *You* dig upon my grave . . .
　Why flashed it not on me
That one true heart was left behind!
What feeling do we ever find
To equal among human kind
　A dog's fidelity!"

"Mistress, I dug upon your grave
　To bury a bone, in case
I should be hungry near this spot
When passing on my daily trot.
I am sorry, but I quite forgot
　It was your resting-place."

IN TENEBRIS

by THOMAS HARDY

"Considerabam ad dexteram, et videbam; et non erat qui cognosceret me . . . Non est qui requirat animam meam."—*Ps. cxlii.*

When the cloud's swoln bosoms echo back the shouts of the many and strong
That things are all as they best may be, save a few to be right ere long,
And my eyes have not the vision in them to discern what to these is so clear
The blot seems straightway in me alone; one better he were not here.

The stout upstanders say, All's well with us; ruers have nought to rue!
And what the potent say so oft, can it fail to be somewhat true?
Breezily go they, breezily come; their dust smokes around their career,
Till I think I am one born out of due time, who has no calling here.

Their dawns bring lusty joys it seems; their evenings all that is sweet;
Our times are blessed times, they cry: Life shapes it as is most meet,
And nothing is much the matter; there are many smiles to a tear;
Then what is the matter is I, I say. Why should such an one be here? . . .

Let him in whose ears the low-voiced Best is killed by the clash of the First,
Who holds that if way to the Better there be, it exacts a full look at the Worst,
Who feels that delight is a delicate growth cramped by crookedness, custom, and fear,
Get him up and be gone as one shaped awry; he disturbs the order here.

TO AN UNBORN PAUPER CHILD

by THOMAS HARDY

I

Breathe not, hid Heart: cease silently,
And though thy birth-hour beckons thee,
Sleep the long sleep:
The Doomsters heap
Travails and teens around us here,
And Time-wraiths turn our songsingings to fear.

II

Hark, how the peoples surge and sigh,
And laughters fail, and greetings die:
Hopes dwindle; yea,
Faiths waste away,
Affections and enthusiasms numb;
Thou canst not mend these things if thou dost come.

III

Had I the ear of wombèd souls
Ere their terrestrial chart unrolls,
And thou wert free
To cease, or be,
Then would I tell thee all I know,
And put it to thee: wilt thou take Life so?

IV

Vain vow! No hint of mine may hence
To theeward fly; to thy locked sense

[653]

Explain none can
Life's pending plan:
Thou will thy ignorant entry make
Though skies spout fire and blood and nations quake.

v

Fain would I, dear, find some shut plot
Of earth's wide wold for thee, where not
One tear, one qualm,
Should break the calm.
But I am weak as thou and bare;
No man can change the common lot to rare.

VI

Must come and bide. And such are we—
Unreasoning, sanguine, visionary—
That I can hope
Health, love, friends, scope
In full for thee; can dream thou wilt find
Joys seldom yet attained by humankind!

THE OXEN

by THOMAS HARDY

Christmas Eve, and twelve of the clock.
"Now they are all on their knees,"
An elder said as we sat in a flock
By the embers in hearthside ease.

We pictured the meek mild creatures where
They dwelt in their strawy pen,
Nor did it occur to one of us there
To doubt they were kneeling then.

So fair a fancy few would weave
In these years! Yet, I feel,
If someone said on Christmas Eve,
"Come; see the oxen kneel,

Afterwards

"In the lonely barton by yonder coomb
   Our childhood used to know,"
I should go with him in the gloom,
   Hoping it might be so.

AFTERWARDS

by THOMAS HARDY

When the Present has latched its postern behind my tremulous stay,
   And the May month flaps its glad green leaves like wings,
Delicate-filmed as new-spun silk, will the neighbors say,
   "He was a man who used to notice such things"?

If it be in the dusk when, like an eyelid's soundless blink,
   The dewfall-hawk comes crossing the shades to alight
Upon the wind-warped upland thorn, a gazer may think,
   "To him this must have been a familiar sight."

If I pass during some nocturnal blackness, mothy and warm,
   When the hedgehog travels furtively over the lawn,
One may say, "He strove that such innocent creatures should come to no harm,
   But he could do little for them; and now he is gone."

If, when hearing that I have been stilled at last, they stand at the door,
   Watching the full-starred heavens that winter sees,
Will this thought rise on those who will meet my face no more,
   "He was one who had an eye for such mysteries"?

And will any say when my bell of quittance is heard in the gloom,
   And a crossing breeze cuts a pause in its outrollings,
Till they rise again, as they were a new bell's boom,
   "He hears it not now, but used to notice such things"?

from THE NAME AND NATURE OF POETRY

by A. E. HOUSMAN

POETRY indeed seems to me more physical than intellectual. A year or two ago, in common with others, I received from America a request that I would define poetry. I replied that I could no more define poetry than a terrier can define a rat, but that I thought we both recognized the object by the symptoms it provokes in us. One of these symptoms was described in connection with another object by Eliphaz the Temanite: "A spirit passed before my face: the hair of my flesh stood up." Experience has taught me, while I am shaving of a morning, to keep watch over my thoughts, because, if a line of poetry strays into my memory, my skin bristles so that the razor ceases to act. This particular symptom is accompanied by a shiver down the spine; there is another which consists in a constriction of the throat and a precipitation of water to the eyes; and there is a third which I can only describe by borrowing a phrase from one of Keats's last letters, where he says, speaking of Fanny Brawne, "everything that reminds me of her goes through me like a spear." The seat of this sensation is the pit of the stomach.

My opinions on poetry are necessarily tinged, perhaps I should say tainted, by the circumstance that I have come into contact with it on two sides. We were saying a while ago that poetry is a very wide term, and inconveniently comprehensive: so comprehensive is it that it embraces two books, fortunately not large ones, of my own. I know how this stuff came into existence; and though I have no right to assume that any other poetry

came into existence in the same way, yet I find reason to believe that some poetry, and quite good poetry, did. Wordsworth for instance says that poetry is the spontaneous overflow of powerful feelings, and Burns has left us this confession, "I have two or three times in my life composed from the wish rather than the impulse, but I never succeeded to any purpose." In short I think that the production of poetry, in its first stage, is less an active than a passive and involuntary process; and if I were obliged, not to define poetry, but to name the class of things to which it belongs, I should call it a secretion; whether a natural secretion, like turpentine in the fir, or a morbid secretion, like the pearl in the oyster, I think that my own case, though I may not deal with the material so cleverly as the oyster does, is the latter; because I have seldom written poetry unless I was rather out of health, and the experience, though pleasurable, was generally agitating and exhausting. If only that you may know what to avoid, I will give some account of the process.

Having drunk a pint of beer at luncheon—beer is a sedative to the brain, and my afternoons are the least intellectual portion of my life—I would go out for a walk of two or three hours. As I went along, thinking of nothing in particular, only looking at things around me and following the progress of the seasons, there would flow into my mind, with sudden and unaccountable emotion, sometimes a line or two of verse, sometimes a whole stanza at once, accompanied, not preceded, by a vague notion of the poem which they

From A. E. Housman, *The Name and Nature of Poetry.* By permission of The Macmillan Company, publishers.

were destined to form part of. Then there would usually be a lull of an hour or so, then perhaps the spring would bubble up again. I say bubble up because, so far as I could make out, the source of the suggestions thus proffered to the brain was an abyss which I have already had occasion to mention, the pit of the stomach. When I got home I wrote them down, leaving gaps, and hoping that further inspiration might be forthcoming another day. Sometimes it was, if I took my walks in a receptive and expectant frame of mind; but sometimes the poem had to be taken in hand and completed by the brain, which was apt to be a matter of trouble and anxiety, involving trial and disappointment, and sometimes ending in failure. I happen to remember distinctly the genesis of the piece which stands last in my first volume. Two of the stanzas, I do not say which, came into my head, just as they are printed, while I was crossing the corner of Hampstead Heath between the Spaniard's Inn and the footpath to Temple Fortune. A third stanza came with a little coaxing after tea. One more was needed, but it did not come: I had to turn to and compose it myself, and that was a laborious business. I wrote it thirteen times, and it was more than a twelvemonth before I got it right.

SOLDIER FROM THE WARS RETURNING

by A. E. Housman

Soldier from the wars returning,
  Spoiler of the taken town,
Here is ease that asks not earning;
  Turn you in and sit you down.

Peace is come and wars are over,
  Welcome you and welcome all,
While the charger crops the clover
  And his bridle hangs in stall.

Now no more of winters biting,
  Filth in trench from fall to spring,
Summers full of sweat and fighting
  For the Kesar or the King.

Rest you, charger, rust you, bridle;
  Kings and kesars, keep your pay;
Soldier, sit you down and idle
  At the inn of night for aye.

THE HALF-MOON WESTERS LOW, MY LOVE

by A. E. Housman

The half-moon westers low, my love,
  And the wind brings up the rain;
And wide apart lie we, my love,
  And seas between the twain.

I know not if it rains, my love,
  In the land where you do lie;
And oh, so sound you sleep, my love,
  You know no more than I.

Poems on pages 621-625 from A. E. Housman, *Collected Poems*, Henry Holt and Company, Inc.

THINK NO MORE, LAD

by A. E. HOUSMAN

Think no more, lad; laugh, be jolly:
  Why should men make haste to die?
Empty heads and tongues a-talking
Make the rough road easy walking,
And the feather pate of folly
  Bears the falling sky.

Oh, 'tis jesting, dancing, drinking
  Spins the heavy world around.
If young hearts were not so clever,
Oh, they would be young for ever:
Think no more; 'tis only thinking
  Lays lads underground.

THE LAWS OF GOD, THE LAWS OF MAN

by A. E. HOUSMAN

The laws of God, the laws of man,
He may keep that will and can;
Not I: let God and man decree
Laws for themselves and not for me;
And if my ways are not as theirs
Let them mind their own affairs.
Their deeds I judge and much condemn
Yet when did I make laws for them?
Please yourselves, say I, and they
Need only look the other way.
But no, they will not; they must still
Wrest their neighbour to their will,

And make me dance as they desire
With jail and gallows and hell-fire.
And how am I to face the odds
Of man's bedevilment and God's?
I, a stranger and afraid
In a world I never made.
They will be master, right or wrong;
Though both are foolish, both are strong.
And since, my soul, we cannot fly
To Saturn nor to Mercury,
Keep we must, if keep we can,
These foreign laws of God and man.

THE CHESTNUT CASTS HIS FLAMBEAUX

by A. E. HOUSMAN

The chestnut casts his flambeaux, and the flowers
  Stream from the hawthorn on the wind away,
The doors clap to, the pane is blind with showers.
  Pass me the can, lad; there's an end of May.

These poems from A. E. Housman, *Last Poems,* Henry Holt and Company, Inc.

"Terence, This Is Stupid Stuff"

There's one spoilt spring to scant our mortal lot,
  One season ruined of our little store.
May will be fine next year as like as not:
  Oh ay, but then we shall be twenty-four.

We for a certainty are not the first
  Have sat in taverns while the tempest hurled
Their hopeful plans to emptiness, and cursed
  Whatever brute and blackguard made the world.

It is in truth iniquity on high
  To cheat our sentenced souls of aught they crave,
And mar the merriment as you and I
  Fare on our long fool's-errand to the grave.

Iniquity it is; but pass the can.
  My lad, no pair of kings our mothers bore;
Our only portion is the estate of man:
  We want the moon, but we shall get no more.

If here to-day the cloud of thunder lours
  To-morrow it will hie on far behests;
The flesh will grieve on other bones than ours
  Soon, and the soul will mourn in other breasts.

The troubles of our proud and angry dust
  Are from eternity, and shall not fail.
Bear them we can, and if we can we must.
  Shoulder the sky, my lad, and drink your ale.

"TERENCE, THIS IS STUPID STUFF"

by A. E. Housman

"Terence, this is stupid stuff:
You eat your victuals fast enough;
There can't be much amiss, 'tis clear,
To see the rate you drink your beer.
But oh, good Lord, the verse you make,
It gives a chap the belly-ache.
The cow, the old cow, she is dead;
It sleeps well, the hornèd head:
We poor lads, 'tis our turn now
To hear such tunes as killed the cow.

Pretty friendship 'tis to rhyme
Your friends to death before their time
Moping melancholy mad:
Come, pipe a tune to dance to, lad."

  Why, if 'tis dancing you would be,
There's brisker pipes than poetry.
Say, for what were hop-yards meant,
Or why was Burton built on Trent?
Oh many a peer of England brews
Livelier liquor than the Muse,

From A. E. Housman, *A Shropshire Lad*, Henry Holt and Company, Inc.

And malt does more than Milton can
To justify God's ways to man.
Ale, man, ale's the stuff to drink
For fellows whom it hurts to think:
Look into the pewter pot
To see the world as the world's not.
And faith, 'tis pleasant till 'tis past:
The mischief is that 'twill not last.
Oh I have been to Ludlow fair
And left my necktie God knows where,
And carried half-way home, or near,
Pints and quarts of Ludlow beer:
Then the world seemed none so bad,
And I myself a sterling lad;
And down in lovely muck I've lain,
Happy till I woke again.
Then I saw the morning sky:
Heigho, the tale was all a lie;
The world, it was the old world yet,
I was I, my things were wet,
And nothing now remained to do
But begin the game anew.

Therefore, since the world has still
Much good, but much less good than ill,
And while the sun and moon endure
Luck's a chance, but trouble's sure,
I'd face it as a wise man would,
And train for ill and not for good.

'Tis true, the stuff I bring for sale
Is not so brisk a brew as ale:
Out of a stem that scored the hand
I wrung it in a weary land.
But take it: if the smack is sour,
The better for the embittered hour;
It should do good to heart and head
When your soul is in my soul's stead;
And I will friend you, if I may,
In the dark and cloudy day.

There was a king reigned in the East:
There, when kings will sit to feast,
They get their fill before they think
With poisoned meat and poisoned drink.
He gathered all that springs to birth
From the many-venomed earth;
First a little, thence to more,
He sampled all her killing store;
And easy, smiling, seasoned sound,
Sate the king when healths went round.
They put arsenic in his meat
And stared aghast to watch him eat;
They poured strychnine in his cup
And shook to see him drink it up:
They shook, they stared as white's their
    shirt:
Them it was their poison hurt.
—I tell the tale that I heard told.
Mithridates, he died old.

WHEN I WAS ONE-AND-TWENTY

by A. E. HOUSMAN

When I was one-and-twenty
  I heard a wise man say,
"Give crowns and pounds and guineas
  But not your heart away;
Give pearls away and rubies
  But keep your fancy free."
But I was one-and-twenty,
  No use to talk to me.

When I was one-and-twenty
  I heard him say again,
"The heart out of the bosom
  Was never given in vain;
'Tis paid with sighs aplenty
  And sold for endless rue."
And I am two-and-twenty,
  And oh, 'tis true, 'tis true.

REVEILLE

by A. E. HOUSMAN

Wake: the silver dusk returning
  Up the beach of darkness brims,
And the ship of sunrise burning
  Strands upon the eastern rims.

Wake: the vaulted shadow shatters,
  Trampled to the floor it spanned,
And the tent of night in tatters
  Straws the sky-pavilioned land.

Up, lad, up, 'tis late for lying:
  Hear the drums of morning play;
Hark, the empty highways crying
  "Who'll beyond the hills away?"

Towns and countries woo together,
  Forelands beacon, belfries call;
Never lad that trod on leather
  Lived to feast his heart with all.

Up, lad: thews that lie and cumber
  Sunlit pallets never thrive;
Morns abed and daylight slumber
  Were not meant for man alive.

Clay lies still, but blood's a rover;
  Breath's a ware that will not keep.
Up, lad: when the journey's over
  There'll be time enough to sleep.

LOVELIEST OF TREES, THE CHERRY NOW

by A. E. HOUSMAN

Loveliest of trees, the cherry now
Is hung with bloom along the bough,
And stands about the woodland ride
Wearing white for Eastertide.

Now, of my threescore years and ten,
Twenty will not come again,

And take from seventy springs a score,
It only leaves me fifty more.

And since to look at things in bloom
Fifty springs are little room,
About the woodlands I will go
To see the cherry hung with snow.

These poems from A. E. Housman, *A Shropshire Lad,* Henry Holt and Company, Inc.

from SELECTED LETTERS

by EDWIN ARLINGTON ROBINSON

Not long ago I attempted . . . to define poetry as "a language that tells us, through a more or less emotional reaction, something that cannot be said." This might be an equally good, or bad, definition of music, but for the fact that the reader would balk instinctively at the qualifying "more or less" before "emotional"—the emotional reaction in the case of music that endures being unquestionably "more." And this, no doubt, is equally true of much of the best poetry . . . poetry is language and music at the same time.*

There is no "philosophy" in my poetry beyond an implication of an ordered universe and a sort of deterministic negation of the general futility that appears to be the basis of "rational" thought. So I suppose you will have to put me down as a mystic, if that means a man who cannot prove all his convictions to be true.*

The world is not a "prison house" but a kind of spiritual kindergarten, where millions of bewildered infants are trying to spell God with the wrong blocks.

—*from The Bookman*

CREDO

by EDWIN ARLINGTON ROBINSON

I cannot find my way: there is no star
In all the shrouded heavens anywhere;
And there is not a whisper in the air
Of any living voice but one so far
That I can hear it only as a bar
Of lost, imperial music, played when fair
And angel fingers wove, and unaware,
Dead leaves to garlands where no roses are.

No, there is not a glimmer, nor a call,
For one that welcomes, welcomes when he fears,
The black and awful chaos of the night;
For through it all—above, beyond it all—
I know the far-sent message of the years,
I feel the coming glory of the Light.

MR. FLOOD'S PARTY

by EDWIN ARLINGTON ROBINSON

Old Eben Flood, climbing alone one night
Over the hill between the town below
And the forsaken upland hermitage
That held as much as he should ever know
On earth again of home, paused warily.
The road was his with not a native near;
And Eben, having leisure, said aloud,
For no man else in Tilbury Town to hear:

"Well, Mr. Flood, we have the harvest
   moon
Again, and we may not have many more;
The bird is on the wing, the poet says,
And you and I have said it here before.
Drink to the bird." He raised up to the
   light
The jug that he had gone so far to fill,
And answered huskily: "Well, Mr. Flood,
Since you propose it, I believe I will."

Alone, as if enduring to the end
A valiant armor of scarred hopes outworn,
He stood there in the middle of the road
Like Roland's ghost winding a silent horn.
Below him, in the town among the trees,
Where friends of other days had honored
   him,
A phantom salutation of the dead
Rang thinly till old Eben's eyes were dim.

Then, as a mother lays her sleeping child
Down tenderly, fearing it may awake,
He set the jug down slowly at his feet
With trembling care, knowing that most
   things break;
And only when assured that on firm earth
It stood, as the uncertain lives of men

Assuredly did not, he paced away,
And with his hand extended paused again:

"Well, Mr. Flood, we have not met like
   this
In a long time; and many a change has
   come
To both of us, I fear, since last it was
We had a drop together. Welcome home!"
Convivially returning with himself,
Again he raised the jug up to the light;
And with an acquiescent quaver said:
"Well, Mr. Flood, if you insist, I might.

"Only a very little, Mr. Flood—
For auld lang syne. No more, sir; that
   will do."
So, for the time, apparently it did,
And Eben evidently thought so too;
For soon amid the silver loneliness
Of night he lifted up his voice and sang,
Secure, with only two moons listening,
Until the whole harmonious landscape
   rang—

"For auld lang syne." The weary throat
   gave out,
The last word wavered, and the song was
   done.
He raised again the jug regretfully
And shook his head, and was again alone.
There was not much that was ahead of
   him,
And there was nothing in the town be-
   low—
Where strangers would have shut the
   many doors
That many friends had opened long ago.

From E. A. Robinson, *Collected Poems.* By permission of The Macmillan Company, publishers.

SONNET

by EDWIN ARLINGTON ROBINSON

Never until our souls are strong enough
To plunge into the crater of the Scheme—
Triumphant in the flash there to redeem
Love's handsel and forevermore to slough,
Like cerements at a played-out masque, the rough
And reptile skins of us whereon we set
The stigma of scared years—are we to get
Where atoms and the ages are one stuff.

Nor ever shall we know the cursed waste
Of life in the beneficence divine
Of starlight and of sunlight and soul-shine
That we have squandered in sin's frail distress,
Till we have drunk, and trembled at the taste,
The mead of Thought's prophetic endlessness.

THE MILL

by EDWIN ARLINGTON ROBINSON

The miller's wife had waited long,
  The tea was cold, the fire was dead;
And there might yet be nothing wrong
  In how he went and what he said:
"There are no millers any more,"
  Was all that she had heard him say;
And he had lingered at the door
  So long that it seemed yesterday.

Sick with a fear that had no form
  She knew that she was there at last;
And in the mill there was a warm
  And mealy fragrance of the past.

What else there was would only seem
  To say again what he had meant;
And what was hanging from a beam
  Would not have heeded where she went

And if she thought it followed her,
  She may have reasoned in the dark
That one way of the few there were
  Would hide her and would leave no
    mark:
Black water, smooth above the weir
  Like starry velvet in the night,
Though ruffled once, would soon appear
  The same as ever to the sight.

From E. A. Robinson, *Collected Poems.* By permission of The Macmillan Company, publishers.

RICHARD CORY

by EDWIN ARLINGTON ROBINSON

Whenever Richard Cory went down town,
   We people on the pavement looked at him:
He was a gentleman from sole to crown,
   Clean favored, and imperially slim.

And he was always quietly arrayed,
   And he was always human when he talked;
But still he fluttered pulses when he said,
   "Good-morning," and he glittered when he walked.

And he was rich—yes, richer than a king,
   And admirably schooled in every grace:
In fine, we thought that he was everything
   To make us wish that we were in his place.

So on we worked, and waited for the light,
   And went without the meat, and cursed the bread;
And Richard Cory, one calm summer night,
   Went home and put a bullet through his head.

From Edwin Arlington Robinson, *The Children of the Night;* used by permission of the publishers, Charles Scribner's Sons.

FLAMMONDE

by EDWIN ARLINGTON ROBINSON

The man Flammonde, from God knows
   where,
With firm address and foreign air,
With news of nations in his talk
And something royal in his walk,
With glint of iron in his eyes,
But never doubt, nor yet surprise,
Appeared, and stayed, and held his head
As one by kings accredited.

Erect, with his alert repose
About him, and about his clothes,
He pictured all tradition hears
Of what we owe to fifty years.
His cleansing heritage of taste
Paraded neither want nor waste;
And what he needed for his fee
To live, he borrowed graciously.

From E. A. Robinson, *Collected Poems.* By permission of The Macmillan Company, publishers.

He never told us what he was,
Or what mischance, or other cause,
Had banished him from better days
To play the Prince of Castaways.
Meanwhile he played surpassing well
A part, for most, unplayable;
In fine, one pauses, half afraid
To say for certain that he played.

For that, one may as well forego
Conviction as to yes or no;
Nor can I say just how intense
Would then have been the difference
To several, who, having striven
In vain to get what he was given,
Would see the stranger taken on
By friends not easy to be won.

Moreover, many a malcontent
He soothed and found munificent;
His courtesy beguiled and foiled
Suspicion that his years were soiled;
His mien distinguished any crowd,
His credit strengthened when he bowed;
And women, young and old, were fond
Of looking at the man Flammonde.

There was a woman in our town
On whom the fashion was to frown;
But while our talk renewed the tinge
Of a long-faded scarlet fringe,
The man Flammonde saw none of that,
And what he saw we wondered at—
That none of us, in her distress,
Could hide or find our littleness.

There was a boy that all agreed
Had shut within him the rare seed
Of learning. We could understand,
But none of us could lift a hand.
The man Flammonde appraised the youth,
And told a few of us the truth;
And thereby, for a little gold,
A flowered future was unrolled.

There were two citizens who fought
For years and years, and over nought;
They made life awkward for their friends,
And shortened their own dividends.
The man Flammonde said what was
    wrong
Should be made right; nor was it long
Before they were again in line,
And had each other in to dine.

And these I mention are but four
Of many out of many more.
So much for them. But what of him—
So firm in every look and limb?
What small satanic sort of kink
Was in his brain? What broken link
Withheld him from the destinies
That came so near to being his?

What was he, when we came to sift
His meaning, and to note the drift
Of incommunicable ways
That make us ponder while we praise?
Why was it that his charm revealed
Somehow the surface of a shield?
What was it that we never caught?
What was he, and what was he not?

How much it was of him we met
We cannot ever know; nor yet
Shall all he gave us quite atone
For what was his, and his alone;
Nor need we now, since he knew best,
Nourish an ethical unrest:
Rarely at once will nature give
The power to be Flammonde and live.

We cannot know how much we learn
From those who never will return,
Until a flash of unforeseen
Remembrance falls on what has been.
We've each a darkening hill to climb;
And this is why, from time to time
In Tilbury Town, we look beyond
Horizons for the man Flammonde.

THE MASTER

(LINCOLN)

by EDWIN ARLINGTON ROBINSON

A flying word from here and there
Had sown the name at which we sneered,
But soon the name was everywhere,
To be reviled and then revered—
A presence to be loved and feared,
We cannot hide it, or deny
That we, the gentlemen who jeered,
May be forgotten by and by.

He came when days were perilous
And hearts of men were sore beguiled;
And having made his note of us,
He pondered and was reconciled.
Was ever master yet so mild
As he, and so untamable?
We doubted, even when he smiled,
Not knowing what he knew so well.

He knew that undeceiving fate
Would shame us whom he served un-
sought;
He knew that he must wince and wait—
The jest of those for whom he fought;
He knew devoutly what he thought
Of us and of our ridicule;
He knew that we must all be taught
Like little children in a school.

We gave a glamour to the task
That he encountered and saw through;
But little of us did he ask,
And little did we ever do.
And what appears if we review
The season when we railed and chaffed?—
It is the face of one who knew
That we were learning while we laughed.

The face that in our vision feels
Again the venom that we flung,
Transfigured to the world reveals
The vigilance to which we clung.
Shrewd, hallowed, harassed, and among
The mysteries that are untold—
The face we see was never young,
Nor could it wholly have been old.

For he, to whom we had applied
Our shopman's test of age and worth,
Was elemental when he died,
As he was ancient at his birth:
The saddest among kings of earth,
Bowed with a galling crown, this man
Met rancor with a cryptic mirth,
Laconic—and Olympian.

The love, the grandeur, and the fame
Are bounded by the world alone;
The calm, the smoldering, and the flame
Of awful patience were his own:
With him they are forever flown
Past all our fond self-shadowings,
Wherewith we cumber the Unknown
As with inept, Icarian wings.

For we were not as other men:
'Twas ours to soar and his to see;
But we are coming down again,
And we shall come down pleasantly;
Nor shall we longer disagree
On what it is to be sublime,
But flourish in our perigee
And have one Titan at a time.

Weary of the Truth

Marsden Hartley
Courtesy Whitney Museum
of American Art

from "THE FIGURE A POEM MAKES"

by ROBERT FROST

The figure a poem makes. It begins in delight and ends in wisdom. The figure is the same as for love. No one can really hold that the ecstasy should be static and stand still in one place. It begins in delight, it inclines to the impulse, it assumes direction with the first line laid down, it runs a course of lucky events, and ends in a clarification of life—not necessarily a great clarification, such as sects and cults are founded on, but in a momentary stay against confusion. It has denouement. It has an outcome that though unforeseen was predestined from the first image of the original mood—and indeed from the very mood. It is but a trick poem and no poem at all if the best of it was thought of first and saved for the last. It finds its own name as it goes and discovers the best waiting for it in some final phrase at once wise and sad— the happy-sad blend of the drinking song.

No tears in the writer, no tears in the reader. No surprise for the writer, no surprise for the reader. For me the initial delight is in the surprise of remembering something I didn't know I knew. I am in a place, a situation, as if I had materialized from cloud or risen out of the ground. There is a glad recognition of the long lost and the rest follows. Step by step the wonder of unexpected supply keeps growing. The impressions most useful to my purpose seem always those I was unaware of and so made no note of at the time when taken, and the conclusion is come to that like giants we are always hurling experience ahead of us to pave the future with against the day when we may want to strike a line of purpose across it for somewhere. The line will have the more charm for not being mechanically straight. We enjoy the straight crookedness of a good walking stick. . . .

More than once I should have lost my soul to radicalism if it had been the originality it was mistaken for by its young converts. Originality and initiative are what I ask for my country. For myself, the originality need be no more than the freshness of a poem run in the way I have described: from delight to wisdom. The figure is the same as for love. Like a piece of ice on a hot stove the poem must ride on its own melting. A poem may be worked over once it is in being, but may not be worried into being. Its most precious quality will remain its having run itself and carried away the poet with it.

TWO TRAMPS IN MUD TIME

by ROBERT FROST

Out of the mud two strangers came	I knew pretty well why he dropped behind
And caught me splitting wood in the yard.	And let the other go on a way.
And one of them put me off my aim	I knew pretty well what he had in mind:
By hailing cheerily 'Hit them hard!'	He wanted to take my job for pay.

Good blocks of beech it was I split,
As large around as the chopping block;
And every piece I squarely hit
Fell splinterless as a cloven rock.
The blows that a life of self-control
Spares to strike for the common good
That day, giving a loose to my soul,
I spent on the unimportant wood.

The sun was warm but the wind was chill.
You know how it is with an April day
When the sun is out and the wind is still,
You're one month on in the middle of May.
But if you so much as dare to speak,
A cloud comes over the sunlit arch,
A wind comes off a frozen peak,
And you're two months back in the middle of March.

A bluebird comes tenderly up to alight
And fronts the wind to unruffle a plume,
His song so pitched as not to excite
A single flower as yet to bloom.
It is snowing a flake: and he half knew
Winter was only playing possum.
Except in color he isn't blue,
But he wouldn't advise a thing to blossom.

The water for which we may have to look
In summertime with a witching-wand,
In every wheelrut's now a brook,
In every print of a hoof a pond.
Be glad of water, but don't forget
The lurking frost in the earth beneath
That will steal forth after the sun is set
And show on the water its crystal teeth.

The time when most I loved my task
These two must make me love it more
By coming with what they came to ask.
You'd think I never had felt before
The weight of an ax-head poised aloft,
The grip on earth of outspread feet,
The life of muscles rocking soft
And smooth and moist in vernal heat.

Out of the woods two hulking tramps
(From sleeping God knows where last night,
But not long since in the lumber camps).
They thought all chopping was theirs of right.
Men of the woods and lumberjacks,
They judged me by their appropriate tool.
Except as a fellow handled an ax,
They had no way of knowing a fool.

Nothing on either side was said.
They knew they had but to stay their stay
And all their logic would fill my head:
As that I had no right to play
With what was another man's work for gain.
My right might be love but theirs was need.
And where the two exist in twain
Theirs was the better right—agreed.

But yield who will to their separation,
My object in living is to unite
My avocation and my vocation
As my two eyes make one in sight.
Only where love and need are one,
And the work is play for mortal stakes,
Is the deed ever really done
For Heaven and the future's sakes.

THE LOCKLESS DOOR
by ROBERT FROST

It went many years,
But at last came a knock,
And I thought of the door
With no lock to lock.

I blew out the light,
I tip-toed the floor,
And raised both hands
In prayer to the door.

But the knock came again.
My window was wide;

I climbed on the sill
And descended outside.

Back over the sill
I bade a 'Come in'
To whatever the knock
At the door may have been.

So at a knock
I emptied my cage
To hide in the world
And alter with age.

THE STAR-SPLITTER
by ROBERT FROST

"You know Orion always comes up sideways.
Throwing a leg up over our fence of mountains,
And rising on his hands, he looks in on me
Busy outdoors by lantern-light with something
I should have done by daylight, and indeed,
After the ground is frozen, I should have done
Before it froze, and a gust flings a handful
Of waste leaves at my smoky lantern chimney
To make fun of my way of doing things,
Or else fun of Orion's having caught me.
Has a man, I should like to ask, no rights
These forces are obliged to pay respect to?"
So Brad McLaughlin mingled reckless talk
Of heavenly stars with hugger-mugger farming,
Till having failed at hugger-mugger farming,
He burned his house down for the fire insurance
And spent the proceeds on a telescope
To satisfy a life-long curiosity
About our place among the infinities.

"What do you want with one of those blame things?"
I asked him well beforehand. "Don't you get one!"
"Don't call it blamed; there isn't anything
More blameless in the sense of being less
A weapon in our human fight," he said.
"I'll have one if I sell my farm to buy it."
There where he moved the rocks to plow the ground
And plowed between the rocks he couldn't move,
Few farms changed hands; so rather than spend years
Trying to sell his farm and then not selling,
He burned his house down for the fire insurance
And bought the telescope with what it came to.
He had been heard to say by several:
"The best thing that we're put here for's to see:
The strongest thing that's given us to see with's
A telescope. Someone in every town
Seems to me owes it to the town to keep one.
In Littleton it may as well be me."
After such loose talk it was no surprise
When he did what he did and burned his house down.

Mean laughter went about the town that day
To let him know we weren't the least imposed on,
And he could wait—we'd see to him to-morrow.
But the first thing next morning we reflected
If one by one we counted people out
For the least sin, it wouldn't take us long
To get so we had no one left to live with.
For to be social is to be forgiving.
Our thief, the one who does our stealing from us,
We don't cut off from coming to church suppers,
But what we miss we go to him and ask for.
He promptly gives it back, that is if still
Uneaten, unworn out, or undisposed of.
It wouldn't do to be too hard on Brad
About his telescope. Beyond the age
Of being given one's gift for Christmas,
He had to take the best way he knew how
To find himself in one. Well, all we said was
He took a strange thing to be roguish over.
Some sympathy was wasted on the house,
A good old-timer dating back along;
But a house isn't sentient; the house
Didn't feel anything. And if it did,

Why not regard it as a sacrifice,
And an old-fashioned sacrifice by fire,
Instead of a new-fashioned one at auction?

Out of a house and so out of a farm
At one stroke (of a match), Brad had to turn
To earn a living on the Concord railroad,
As under-ticket-agent at a station
Where his job, when he wasn't selling tickets,
Was setting out up track and down, not plants
As on a farm, but planets, evening stars
That varied in their hue from red to green.

He got a good glass for six hundred dollars.
His new job gave him leisure for star-gazing.
Often he bid me come and have a look
Up the brass barrel, velvet black inside,
At a star quaking in the other end.
I recollect a night of broken clouds
And underfoot snow melted down to ice,
And melting further in the wind to mud.
Bradford and I had out the telescope.
We spread our two legs as we spread its three,
Pointed our thoughts the way we pointed it,
And standing at our leisure till the day broke,
Said some of the best things we ever said.
That telescope was christened the Star-splitter,
Because it didn't do a thing but split
A star in two or three the way you split
A globule of quicksilver in your hand
With one stroke of your finger in the middle.
It's a star-splitter if there ever was one
And ought to do some good if splitting stars
'Sa thing to be compared with splitting wood.

We've looked and looked, but after all where are we?
Do we know any better where we are,
And how it stands between the night to-night
And a man with a smoky lantern chimney?
How different from the way it ever stood?

DEPARTMENTAL

by ROBERT FROST

An ant on the table cloth
Ran into a dormant moth
Of many times his size.
He showed not the least surprise.
His business wasn't with such.
He gave it scarcely a touch,
And was off on his duty run.
Yet if he encountered one
Of the hive's enquiry squad
Whose work is to find out God
And the nature of time and space,
He would put him onto the case.
Ants are a curious race;
One crossing with hurried tread
The body of one of their dead
Isn't given a moment's arrest—
Seems not even impressed.
But he no doubt reports to any
With whom he crosses antennae,
And they no doubt report
To the higher up at court.

Then word goes forth in Formic:
"Death's come to Jerry McCormic,
Our selfless forager Jerry.
Will the special Janizary
Whose office it is to bury
The dead of the commissary
Go bring him home to his people.
Lay him in state on a sepal.
Wrap him for shroud in a petal.
Embalm him with ichor of nettle.
This is the word of your Queen."
And presently on the scene
Appears a solemn mortician;
And taking formal position
With feelers calmly atwiddle,
Seizes the dead by the middle,
And heaving him high in the air,
Carries him out of there.
No one stands round to stare.
It is nobody else's affair.

It couldn't be called ungentle.
But how thoroughly departmental

From Robert Frost, *Collected Poems,* Henry Holt and Company, Inc.

TO A THINKER

by ROBERT FROST

The last step taken found your heft
Decidedly upon the left.
One more would throw you on the right.
Another still—you see your plight.

You call this thinking, but it's walking.
Not even that, it's only rocking,
Or weaving like a stabled horse:
From force to matter and back to force,

n form to content and back to form,
m norm to crazy and back to norm,
om bound to free and back to bound,
om sound to sense, and back to sound.
back and forth. It almost scares
man the way things come in pairs.
Just now you're off democracy
(With a polite regret to be),
And leaning on dictatorship;
But if you will accept the tip,
In less than no time, tongue and pen,
You'll be a democrat again.
A reasoner and good as such,
Don't let it bother you too much

If it makes you look helpless please
And a temptation to the tease.
Suppose you've no direction in you,
I don't see but you must continue
To use the gift you do possess,
And sway with reason more or less.
I own I never really warmed
To the reformer or reformed,
And yet conversion has its place
Not half way down the scale of grace.
So if you find you must repent
From side to side in argument,
At least don't use your mind too hard,
But trust my instinct—I'm a bard.

THE VANTAGE POINT

by ROBERT FROST

If tired of trees I seek again mankind,
    Well I know where to hie me—in the dawn,
    To a slope where the cattle keep the lawn.
There amid lolling juniper reclined,
Myself unseen, I see in white defined
    Far off the homes of men, and farther still,
    The graves of men on an opposing hill,
Living or dead, whichever are to mind.

And if by noon I have too much of these,
    I have but to turn on my arm, and lo,
    The sun-burned hillside sets my face aglow,
My breathing shakes the bluet like a breeze,
    I smell the earth, I smell the bruisèd plant,
    I look into the crater of the ant.

A DRUMLIN WOODCHUCK

by ROBERT FROST

One thing has a shelving bank,
Another a rotting plank,
To give it cozier skies
And make up for its lack of size.

My own strategic retreat
Is where two rocks almost meet,
And still more secure and snug,
A two-door burrow I dug.

With those in mind at my back
I can sit forth exposed to attack
As one who shrewdly pretends
That he and the world are friends.

All we who prefer to live
Have a little whistle we give,
And flash, at the least alarm
We dive down under the farm.

We allow some time for guile
And don't come out for a while
Either to eat or drink.
We take occasion to think.

And if after the hunt goes past
And the double-barrelled blast
(Like war and pestilence
And the loss of common sense),

If I can with confidence say
That still for another day,
Or even another year,
I will be there for you, my dear,

It will be because, though small
As measured against the All,
I have been so instinctively thorough
About my crevice and burrow.

STOPPING BY WOODS ON A SNOWY EVENING

by ROBERT FROST

Whose woods these are I think I know.
His house is in the village though;
He will not see me stopping here
To watch his woods fill up with snow.

My little horse must think it queer
To stop without a farmhouse near
Between the woods and frozen lake
The darkest evening of the year.

He gives his harness bells a shake
To ask if there is some mistake.
The only other sound's the sweep
Of easy wind and downy flake.

The woods are lovely, dark and deep.
But I have promises to keep,
And miles to go before I sleep,
And miles to go before I sleep.

NEITHER OUT FAR NOR IN DEEP

by ROBERT FROST

The people along the sand
All turn and look one way.
They turn their back on the land.
They look at the sea all day.

As long as it takes to pass
A ship keeps raising its hull;
The wetter ground like glass
Reflects a standing gull.

The land may vary more;
But wherever the truth may be—
The water comes ashore,
And the people look at the sea.

They cannot look out far.
They cannot look in deep.
But when was that ever a bar
To any watch they keep?

WEST-RUNNING BROOK

by ROBERT FROST

"Fred, where is north?"

　　　　　　"North? North is there, my love.

The brook runs west."

　　　　　　"West-running Brook then call it."
(West-running Brook men call it to this day.)
"What does it think it's doing running west
When all the other country brooks flow east
To reach the ocean? It must be the brook
Can trust itself to go by contraries
The way I can with you—and you with me—
Because we're—we're—I don't know what we are.
What are we?

　　　　"Young or new?"

　　　　　　"We must be something.
We've said we two. Let's change that to we three.
As you and I are married to each other,
We'll both be married to the brook. We'll build

Our bridge across it, and the bridge shall be
Our arm thrown over it asleep beside it.
Look, look, it's waving to us with a wave
To let us know it hears me."

                "Why, my dear,
That wave's been standing off this jut of shore—"
(The black stream, catching on a sunken rock,
Flung backward on itself in one white wave,
And the white water rode the black forever,
Not gaining but not losing, like a bird
White feathers from the struggle of whose breast
Flecked the dark stream and flecked the darker pool
Below the point, and were at last driven wrinkled
In a white scarf against the far shore alders.)
"That wave's been standing off this jut of shore
Ever since rivers, I was going to say,
Were made in heaven. It wasn't waved to us."

"It wasn't, yet it was. If not to you
It was to me—in an annunciation."

"Oh, if you take it off to lady-land,
As't were the country of the Amazons
We men must see you to the confines of
And leave you there, ourselves forbid to enter,—
It is your brook! I have no more to say."

"Yes, you have, too. Go on. You thought of something."

"Speaking of contraries, see how the brook
In that white wave runs counter to itself.
It is from that in water we were from
Long, long before we were from any creature.
Here we, in our impatience of the steps,
Get back to the beginning of beginnings,
The stream of everything that runs away.
Some say existence like a Pirouot
And Pirouette, forever in one place,
Stands still and dances, but it runs away,
It seriously, sadly, runs away
To fill the abyss' void with emptiness.
It flows beside us in this water brook,
But it flows over us. It flows between us
To separate us for a panic moment.

Fire and Ice

It flows between us, over us, and *with* us.
And it is time, strength, tone, light, life and love—
And even substance lapsing unsubstantial;
The universal cataract of death
That spends to nothingness—and unresisted,
Save by some strange resistance in itself,
Not just a swerving, but a throwing back,
As if regret were in it and were sacred.
It has this throwing backward on itself
So that the fall of most of it is always
Raising a little, sending up a little.
Our life runs down in sending up the clock.
The brook runs down in sending up our life.
The sun runs down in sending up the brook.
And there is something sending up the sun.
It is this backward motion toward the source,
Against the stream, that most we see ourselves in,
The tribute of the current to the source.
It is from this in nature we are from.
It is most us."

        "Today will be the day
You said so."

        "No, today will be the day
You said the brook was called West-running Brook."

"Today will be the day of what we both said."

FIRE AND ICE

by ROBERT FROST

Some say the world will end in fire,
Some say in ice.
From what I've tasted of desire
I hold with those who favor fire.
But if it had to perish twice,

I think I know enough of hate
To know that for destruction ice
Is also great
And would suffice.

MENDING WALL
by ROBERT FROST

Something there is that doesn't love a wall,
That sends the frozen-ground-swell under it,
And spills the upper boulders in the sun;
And makes gaps even two can pass abreast.
The work of hunters is another thing:
I have come after them and made repair
Where they have left not one stone on a stone,
But they would have the rabbit out of hiding,
To please the yelping dogs. The gaps I mean,
No one has seen them made or heard them made,
But at spring mending-time we find them there.
I let my neighbour know beyond the hill;
And on a day we meet to walk the line
And set the wall between us once again.
We keep the wall between us as we go.
To each the boulders that have fallen to each.
And some are loaves and some so nearly balls
We have to use a spell to make them balance:
"Stay where you are until our backs are turned!"
We wear our fingers rough with handling them.
Oh, just another kind of out-door game,
One on a side. It comes to little more:
There where it is we do not need the wall:
He is all pine and I am apple orchard.
My apple trees will never get across
And eat the cones under his pines, I tell him.
He only says, "Good fences make good neighbours."
Spring is the mischief in me, and I wonder
If I could put a notion in his head:
"*Why* do they make good neighbours? Isn't it
Where there are cows? But here there are no cows.

There Are Roughly Zones

Before I built a wall I'd ask to know
What I was walling in or walling out,
And to whom I was like to give offence.
Something there is that doesn't love a wall,
That wants it down." I could say "Elves" to him,
But it's not elves exactly, and I'd rather
He said it for himself. I see him there,
Bringing a stone grasped firmly by the top
In each hand, like an old-stone savage armed.
He moves in darkness as it seems to me,
Not of woods only and the shade of trees.
He will not go behind his father's saying,
And he likes having thought of it so well
He says again, "Good fences make good neighbours."

THERE ARE ROUGHLY ZONES
by ROBERT FROST

We sit indoors and talk of the cold outside.
And every gust that gathers strength and heaves
Is a threat to the house. But the house has long been tried.
We think of the tree. If it never again has leaves,
We'll know, we say, that this was the night it died.
It is very far north, we admit, to have brought the peach.
What comes over a man, is it soul or mind—
That to no limits and bounds he can stay confined?
You would say his ambition was to extend the reach
Clear to the Arctic of every living kind.
Why is his nature forever so hard to teach
That though there is no fixed line between wrong and right,
There are roughly zones whose laws must be obeyed.
There is nothing much we can do for the tree tonight,
But we can't help feeling more than a little betrayed
That the northwest wind should rise to such a height
Just when the cold went down so many below.

The tree has no leaves and may never have them again.
We must wait till some months hence in the spring to know.
But if it is destined never again to grow,
It can blame this limitless trait in the hearts of men.

ACQUAINTED WITH THE NIGHT

by ROBERT FROST

I have been one acquainted with the night.
I have walked out in rain—and back in rain.
I have outwalked the furthest city light.

I have looked down the saddest city lane.
I have passed by the watchman on his beat.
And dropped my eyes, unwilling to explain.

I have stood still and stopped the sound of feet
When far away an interrupted cry
Came over houses from another street,

But not to call me back or say good-bye;
And further still at an unearthly height,
One luminary clock against the sky

Proclaimed the time was neither wrong nor right.
I have been one acquainted with the night.

Nighthawks. Edward Hopper.

Courtesy Art Institute of Chicago

from THE PEOPLE, YES

by CARL SANDBURG

57

Lincoln?
He was a mystery in smoke and flags
saying yes to the smoke, yes to the flags,
yes to the paradoxes of democracy,
yes to the hopes of government
of the people by the people for the people,
no to debauchery of the public mind,
no to personal malice nursed and fed,
yes to the Constitution when a help,
no to the Constitution when a hindrance,
yes to man as a struggler amid illusions,
each man fated to answer for himself:
Which of the faiths and illusions of mankind
must I choose for my own sustaining light
to bring me beyond the present wilderness?

    Lincoln? was he a poet?
    and did he write verses?
"I have not willingly planted a thorn
    in any man's bosom."
"I shall do nothing through malice; what
    I deal with is too vast for malice."

Death was in the air.
So was birth.
What was dying few could say.
What was being born none could know.

He took the wheel in a lashing roaring
    hurricane.
And by what compass did he steer the course
    of the ship?
"My policy is to have no policy," he said in
    the early months,
And three years later, "I have been controlled
    by events."

He could play with the wayward human mind, saying at Charleston, Illinois, September 18, 1858, it was no answer to an argument to call a man a liar.

"I assert that you [pointing a finger in the face of a man in the crowd] are here today, and you undertake to prove me a liar by showing that you were in Mattoon yesterday.

"I say that you took your hat off your head and you prove me a liar by putting it on your head."

He saw personal liberty across wide horizons.

"Our progress in degeneracy appears to me to be pretty rapid," he wrote Joshua F. Speed, August 24, 1855. "As a nation we began by declaring that 'all men are created equal, except Negroes.' When the Know-Nothings get control, it will read 'all men are created equal except Negroes and foreigners and Catholics.' When it comes to this, I shall prefer emigrating to some country where they make no pretense of loving liberty."

> Did he look deep into a crazy pool
> and see the strife and wrangling
> with a clear eye, writing the military
> head of a stormswept area:
> "If both factions, or neither, shall abuse
> you, you will probably be about right. Be-
> ware of being assailed by one and praised
> by the other"?

Lincoln? was he a historian?
did he know mass chaos?
did he have an answer for those
who asked him to organize chaos?

"Actual war coming, blood grows hot, and blood is spilled. Thought is forced from old channels into confusion. Deception breeds and thrives. Confidence dies and universal suspicion reigns.

"Each man feels an impulse to kill his neighbor, lest he be first killed by him. Revenge and retaliation follow. And all this, as before said, may be among honest men only; but this is not all.

"Every foul bird comes abroad and every dirty reptile rises up. These add crime to confusion.

"Strong measures, deemed indispensable, but harsh at best, such men make worse by maladministration. Murders for old grudges, and murders for pelf, proceed under any cloak that will best cover for the occasion. These causes amply account for what has happened in Missouri."

Early in '64 the Committee of the New York Workingman's Democratic Republican Association called on him with assurances and he meditated aloud for them, recalling race and draft riots:

The People, Yes

"The most notable feature of a disturbance in your city last summer was the
hanging of some working people by other working people. It should never
be so.

"The strongest bond of human sympathy, outside of the family relation, should
be one uniting all working people, of all nations and tongues and kindreds.

"Let not him who is houseless pull down the house of another, but let him labor
diligently and build one for himself, thus by example assuring that his own
shall be safe from violence when built."

Lincoln? did he gather
the feel of the American dream
and see its kindred over the earth?

"As labor is the common burden of our race,
so the effort of some to shift
their share of the burden
onto the shoulders of others
is the great durable curse of the race."

"I hold,
if the Almighty had ever made a set of men
that should do all of the eating
and none of the work,
he would have made them
with mouths only, and no hands;
and if he had ever made another class,
that he had intended should do all the work
and none of the eating,
he would have made them
without mouths and all hands."

"—the same spirit that says, 'You toil and
work and earn bread, and I'll eat it.' No
matter in what shape it comes, whether
from the mouth of a king who seeks to
bestride the people of his own nation
and live by the fruit of their labor, or
from one race of men as an apology for
enslaving another race, it is the same
tyrannical principle."

"As I would not be a *slave,* so I would not
be a *master.* This expresses my idea of
democracy. Whatever differs from this,
to the extent of the difference, is no de-
mocracy."

[685]

"I never knew a man who wished to be him-
self a slave. Consider if you know any
good thing that no man desires for him-
self."

"The sheep and the wolf
are not agreed upon a definition
of the word liberty."

"The whole people of this nation
will ever do well
if well done by."

"The plainest print cannot be read
through a gold eagle."

"How does it feel to be President?" an Illi-
nois friend asked.
"Well, I'm like the man they rode out of
town on a rail. He said if it wasn't for
the honor of it he would just as soon
walk."

> Lincoln? he was a dreamer.
> He saw ships at sea,
> he saw himself living and dead
> in dreams that came.

Into a secretary's diary December 23, 1863,
went an entry: "The President tonight
had a dream. He was in a party of plain
people, and, as it became known who
he was, they began to comment on his
appearance. One of them said: 'He is a
very common-looking man.' The Pres-
ident replied: 'The Lord prefers com-
mon-looking people. That is the reason
he makes so many of them.'"

> He spoke one verse for then and now:
> "If we could first know where we are,
> and whither we are tending,
> we could better judge
> what to do, and how to do it."

THE ROSE OF THE WORLD

by WILLIAM BUTLER YEATS

Who dreamed that beauty passes like a dream?
For these red lips with all their mournful pride,
Mournful that no new wonder may betide,
Troy passed away in one high funeral gleam,
And Usna's children died.

We and the laboring world are passing by:
Amid men's souls, that waver and give place,
Like the pale waters in their wintry race,
Under the passing stars, frame of the sky,
Lives on this lonely face.

Bow down, archangels, in your dim abode:
Before you were, or any hearts to beat,
Weary and kind, one lingered by His seat;
He made the world to be a grassy road
Before her wandering feet.

THE SECOND COMING

by WILLIAM BUTLER YEATS

Turning and turning in the widening gyre
The falcon cannot hear the falconer;
Things fall apart; the centre cannot hold;
Mere anarchy is loosed upon the world,
The blood-dimmed tide is loosed, and
  everywhere
The ceremony of innocence is drowned;
The best lack all conviction, while the
  worst
Are full of passionate intensity.

Surely some revelation is at hand;
Surely the Second Coming is at hand.
The Second Coming! Hardly are those
  words out
When a vast image out of *Spiritus Mundi*
Troubles my sight: somewhere in sands
  of the desert
A shape with lion body and the head of a
  man,
A gaze blank and pitiless as the sun,
Is moving its slow thighs, while all about
  it
Reel shadows of the indignant desert birds.
The darkness drops again; but now I
  know
That twenty centuries of stony sleep
Were vexed to nightmare by a rocking
  cradle,
And what rough beast, its hour come
  round at last,
Slouches towards Bethlehem to be born?

LEDA AND THE SWAN

by WILLIAM BUTLER YEATS

A sudden blow: the great wings beating
still
Above the staggering girl, her thighs ca-
ressed
By the dark webs, her nape caught in his
bill,
He holds her helpless breast upon his
breast.

How can those terrified vague fingers push
The feathered glory from her loosening
thighs?
And how can body, laid in that white rush,

But feel the strange heart beating where
it lies?

A shudder in the loins engenders there
The broken wall, the burning roof and
tower
And Agamemnon dead.

          Being so caught up,
So mastered by the brute blood of the air,
Did she put on his knowledge with his
power
Before the indifferent beak could let her
drop?

I think if I could be given a month of Antiquity and leave to spend it where I
chose, I would spend it in Byzantium a little before Justinian opened St. Sophia
and closed the Academy of Plato. I think I could find in some little wine-shop some
philosophical worker in mosaic who could answer all my questions, the supernatural
descending nearer to him than to Plotinus even. . . . I think that in early Byzantium,
maybe never before or since in recorded history, religious, aesthetic and practical life
were one . . .

—A Vision

SAILING TO BYZANTIUM

by WILLIAM BUTLER YEATS

That is no country for old men. The young
In one another's arm, birds in the trees,
—Those dying generations—at their song,
The salmon-falls, the mackerel-crowded seas,
Fish, flesh, or fowl, commend all summer long
Whatever is begotten, born, and dies.
Caught in that sensual music all neglect
Monuments of unageing intellect.

II

An aged man is but a paltry thing,
A tattered coat upon a stick, unless
Soul clap its hands and sing, and louder sing
For every tatter in its mortal dress,
Nor is there singing school but studying
Monuments of its own magnificence;
And therefore I have sailed the seas and come
To the holy city of Byzantium.

III

O sages standing in God's holy fire
As in the gold mosaic of a wall,
Come from the holy fire, perne in a gyre,
And be the singing-masters of my soul.
Consume my heart away; sick with desire
And fastened to a dying animal
It knows not what it is; and gather me
Into the artifice of eternity.

IV

Once out of nature I shall never take
My bodily form from any natural thing,
But such a form as Grecian goldsmiths make
Of hammered gold and gold enamelling
To keep a drowsy Emperor awake;
Or set upon a golden bough to sing
To lords and ladies of Byzantium
Of what is past, or passing, or to come.

BYZANTIUM

by William Butler Yeats

The unpurged images of day recede;
The Emperor's drunken soldiery are abed;
Night resonance recedes, night-walkers' song
After great cathedral gong;
A starlit or a moonlit dome disdains

[689]

All that man is,
All mere complexities,
The fury and the mire of human veins.

Before me floats an image, man or shade,
Shade more than man, more image than a shade;
For Hades' bobbin bound in mummy-cloth
May unwind the winding path;
A mouth that has no moisture and no breath
Breathless mouths may summon;
I hail the superhuman;
I call it death-in-life and life-in-death.

Miracle, bird or golden handiwork,
More miracle than bird or handiwork,
Planted on the starlit golden bough,
Can like the cocks of Hades crow,
Or, by the moon embittered, scorn aloud
In glory of changeless metal
Common bird or petal
And all complexities of mire or blood.

At midnight on the Emperor's pavement flit
Flames that no faggot feeds, nor steel has lit,
Nor storm disturbs, flames begotten of flame,
Where blood-begotten spirits come
And all complexities of fury leave,
Dying into a dance,
An agony of trance,
An agony of flame that cannot singe a sleeve.

Astraddle on the dolphin's mire and blood,
Spirit after spirit! The smithies break the flood,
The golden smithies of the Emperor!
Marbles of the dancing floor
Break bitter furies of complexity,
Those images that yet
Fresh images beget,
That dolphin-torn, that gong-tormented sea.

A NOTE ON BYZANTIUM

In his Diary for April 30, 1930, Yeats wrote: "Subject for a poem . . . Describe Byzantium as it is in the system towards the end of the first Christian millennium. A walking mummy. Flames at the street corners where the soul is purified, birds of hammered gold singing in the golden trees, in the harbour [sic], offering their backs to the wailing dead that they may carry them to paradise." Yeats depicts the spirits of the dead purifying themselves from the impurities of the living. It is night in Byzantium. The impure and unpurged living have withdrawn. The sounds of night have receded, the songs of night-walkers and the sound of the cathedral gong, which is not only a symbol of religious ritual tolling out the living and tolling in the dead, but also of the sensual music of impurities which later torments the sea. A cathedral dome, as of Santa Sophia, is lit by the stars or the moon; that is, during Phase 1 at the dark of the moon, or during Phase 15 when the stars recede in the glare of the full moon. Both are supernatural phases where no human incarnation is possible, for Phase 1 "is a supernatural incarnation, like Phase 15, because there is complete objectivity, and human life cannot be completely objective. At Phase 15 mind was completely absorbed by being, but now body is completely absorbed in its supernatural environment . . . mind and body take whatever shape, accept whatever image is imprinted upon them . . . are indeed the instruments of supernatural manifestation, the final link between the living and more powerful beings."—*A Vision*, p. 183. In this great silence, the starlit or moonlit dome disdains the fury

and mire of human duality. The spirits now begin to float in from the realm of the dead.

Yeats describes various forms which the spirit may take during the second state: "In the *Meditation* it wears the form it had immediately before death; in the *Dreaming Back* and the *Phantasmagoria*, should it appear to the living, it has the form of the dream, in the *Return* the form worn during the event explored, in the *Shiftings* whatever form was most familiar to others during its life; in the *Purification* whatever form it fancies."—*A Vision*, p. 235. The spirits live in Hades; the bobbin, or spindle of Hades, symbolizes the revolving and gyrating motions of the dead undergoing their purifications, and the mummy-cloth is a symbol of their lives revolving on that spindle. Reliving their previous lives in memory, by *Dreaming Back* and in *Return,* they thus unwind a similar natural spindle or gyre of their lives upon earth called the "winding path" so that they may become freed of all natural attributes or memories. Caught in a limbo of air between the Condition of Fire and the terrestrial condition, they receive an inflowing from both directions and must continually shuttle between them. "The inflowing from their mirrored life, who themselves receive it from the Condition of Fire, falls upon the Winding Path called the Path of the Serpent, and that inflowing coming alike to men and to animals is called natural. . . . In so far as a man is like all other men, the inflow finds him upon the winding path, and in so far as he is a saint or sage, upon the straight path." The spirit's "descending power," however, "is neither the winding

By Kimon Friar. From Friar and Brinnin, *Modern Poetry,* copyright, 1951, by Appleton-Century-Crofts, Inc. Reprinted by permission of Appleton-Century-Crofts, Inc.

nor the straight line but zigzag . . . it is the sudden lightning, for all his acts of power are instantaneous. We perceive in the pulsation of the artery, and after slowly decline."—*Essays* (New York, Macmillan, 1924), pp. 528-529. Spirit now calls to spirit, and the poet, himself a spirit having neither the moisture nor the breath of the living, calls upon the superhuman in whom the dualities of life and death are being simultaneously resolved. The poet then turns to images of hammered golden birds wrought by human hands to such artifice that they seem inhuman and miraculous, identical in symbol to the spirits. In starlight these birds can crow like the cocks of Hades, a suggestion that if the spirits of the dead must recede before the crowing of a terrestrial cock, as legend has it, then the unpurged images of the living must recede before the cocks of Hades or the singing artificial birds of Byzantium. They sing of their singleness and changelessness, and scorn the passing, decaying birds and flowers of nature, the evil and passion of human complexity. The poet then turns again to the spirits of flame who in an agony of fire and trance are trying to die out of the complexities of human fury in a flaming dance which symbolizes the underlining rhythmic, gyrating pulse of creation. Since these spirits are composed of spiritual and not physical fire, no faggot can feed them, no flint can ignite them, no storm can disturb them, and they in turn cannot singe anything. They were once begotten out of the complexities of human blood which they must now purge away; also, like the bird who came out of the fire, spirit can beget spirit, flame beget flame "as one candle takes light from another."

In discussing that aspect of the second stage called *Phantasmagoria,* Yeats writes of those spirits that appear under the impulse of moral and emotional suffering, and recounts the story of a Japanese girl whose ghost tells a priest of a slight sin, which seems great to her because of her exaggerated conscience: "She is surrounded by flames, and though the priest explains that if she but ceased to believe in those flames they would cease to exist, believe she must, and the play ends in an elaborate dance, the dance of her agony." —*A Vision,* p. 231. Yeats reports the following conversation between himself and a spirit from the fifth state, that of *Purification:* " 'We have no power,' said an inhabitant of the state, 'except to purify our intention,' and when I asked of what, replied: 'Of complexity.' "—*A Vision,* p. 233. The poet finally turns to a vision of the spirits astraddle on the backs of dolphins plunging in an element of water and who carry them back and forth between the terrestrial condition of the living and the spiritual condition of fire and air. (According to Mrs. Arthur Strong's *Apotheosis and After-Life,* dolphins, in the art of the ancient world, were symbols of the soul and its transit.) The miraculous handiwork of the Byzantium goldsmiths, which are themselves now symbols of spirit, break in upon this spiritual flood, and also, in another sense of "break," transcend, overcome, or defeat the flood. The marble mosaics on the dancing floor of the Emperor's pavement (the Forum of Constantine known as "The Pavement" because of its marble floor), also break in upon and are involved in the dance. Thus the poem ends with a whirling dance broken into fragmented images, images begetting images of both symbol and spirit, and all tossed upon a dolphin-torn and gong-tormented sea of complexity, fury, and blood.

from SELECTED ESSAYS
by T. S. ELIOT

Dante

In my experience of the appreciation of poetry I have always found that the less I knew about the poet and his work, before I began to read it, the better.

Tradition and the Individual Talent

I am alive to a usual objection to what is clearly part of my programme for the *metier* of poetry. The objection is that the doctrine requires a ridiculous amount of erudition (pedantry), a claim which can be rejected by appeal to the lives of poets in any pantheon. It will even be affirmed that much learning deadens or perverts poetic sensibility.

The Metaphysical Poets

It is not a permanent necessity that poets should be interested in philosophy, or in any other subject. We can only say that it appears likely that poets in our civilization, as it exists at present, must be *difficult*. Our civilization comprehends great variety and complexity, and this variety and complexity, playing upon a refined sensibility, must produce various and complex results. The poet must become more and more comprehensive, more allusive, more indirect, in order to force, to dislocate if necessary, language into his meaning.

William Blake

Blake was endowed with a capacity for considerable understanding of human nature with a remarkable and original sense of language, and a gift of hallucinated vision. Had these been controlled by a respect for impersonal reason, for common sense, for the objectivity of science, it would have been better for him.

ANIMULA

by T. S. ELIOT

"Issues from the hand of God, the simple
    soul"
To a flat world of changing lights and
    noise,
To light, dark, dry or damp, chilly or
    warm;
Moving between the legs of tables and of
    chairs,
Rising or falling, grasping at kisses and
    toys,
Advancing boldly, sudden to take alarm,
Retreating to the corner of arm and knee,
Eager to be reassured, taking pleasure
In the fragrant brilliance of the Christmas
    tree,
Pleasure in the wind, the sunlight and the
    sea;
Studies the sunlit pattern on the floor
And running stags around a silver tray;
Confounds the actual and the fanciful,
Content with playing-cards and kings and
    queens,
What the fairies do and what the servants
    say.
The heavy burden of the growing soul
Perplexes and offends more, day by day;
Week by week, offends and perplexes
    more

With the imperatives of "is and seems"
And may and may not, desire and control
The pain of living and the drug of dreams
Curl up the small soul in the window seat
Behind the *Encylopædia Britannica.*
Issues from the hand of time the simple
    soul
Irresolute and selfish, misshapen, lame,
Unable to fare forward or retreat,
Fearing the warm reality, the offered
    good,
Denying the importunity of the blood,
Shadow of its own shadows, specter in its
    own gloom,
Leaving disordered papers in a dusty
    room;
Living first in the silence after the viati-
    cum.

Pray for Guiterriez, avid of speed and
    power,
For Boudin, blown to pieces,
For this one who made a great fortune,
And that one who went his own way.
Pray for Floret, by the boarhound slain
    between the yew trees,
Pray for us now and at the hour of our
    birth.

THE LOVE SONG OF J. ALFRED PRUFROCK
by T. S. Eliot

S'io credesse che mia risposta fosse
A persona che mai tornasse al mondo,
Questa fiamma staria senza piu scosse.
Ma perciocche giammai di questo fondo
Non torno vivo alcun, s'i'odo il vero,
*Senza tema d'infamia ti rispondo.**

Let us go then, you and I,
When the evening is spread out against the sky
Like a patient etherized upon a table;
Let us go, through certain half-deserted streets,
The muttering retreats
Of restless nights in one-night cheap hotels
And sawdust restaurants with oyster-shells:
Streets that follow like a tedious argument
Of insidious intent
To lead you to an overwhelming question. . .
Oh, do not ask, "What is it?"
Let us go and make our visit.

In the room the women come and go
Talking of Michelangelo.

The yellow fog that rubs its back upon the window-panes,
The yellow smoke that rubs its muzzle on the window-panes
Licked its tongue into the corners of the evening,
Lingered upon the pools that stand in drains,

* If I thought my answer were to one who ever could return to the world, this flame should shake no more. But since none ever did return alive from this depth, if what I hear be true, without fear of infamy I answer thee.

Let fall upon its back the soot that falls from chimneys,
Slipped by the terrace, made a sudden leap,
And seeing that it was a soft October night,
Curled once about the house, and fell asleep.

And indeed there will be time
For the yellow smoke that slides along the street,
Rubbing its back upon the window-panes;
There will be time, there will be time
To prepare a face to meet the faces that you meet;
There will be time to murder and create,
And time for all the works and days of hands
That lift and drop a question on your plate;
Time for you and time for me,
And time yet for a hundred indecisions,
And for a hundred visions and revisions,
Before the taking of a toast and tea.

In the room the women come and go
Talking of Michelangelo.

And indeed there will be time
To wonder, "Do I dare?" and, "Do I dare?"
Time to turn back and descend the stair,
With a bald spot in the middle of my hair—
(They will say: "How his hair is growing thin!")
My morning coat, my collar mounting firmly to the chin,
My necktie rich and modest, but asserted by a simple pin—
(They will say: "But how his arms and legs are thin!")
Do I dare
Disturb the universe?
In a minute there is time
For decisions and revisions which a minute will reverse.

For I have known them all already, known them all:—
Have known the evenings, mornings, afternoons,
I have measured out my life with coffee spoons;
I know the voices dying with a dying fall
Beneath the music from a farther room.
    So how should I presume?

And I have known the eyes already, known them all—
The eyes that fix you in a formulated phrase,
And when I am formulated, sprawling on a pin,

The Love Song of J. Alfred Prufrock

When I am pinned and wriggling on the wall,
Then how should I begin
To spit out all the butt-ends of my days and ways?
    And how should I presume?

And I have known the arms already, known them all—
Arms that are braceleted and white and bare
(But in the lamplight, downed with light brown hair!)
Is it perfume from a dress
That makes me so digress?
Arms that lie along a table, or wrap about a shawl.
    And should I then presume?
    And how should I begin?

    .   .   .   .   .   .

Shall I say, I have gone at dusk through narrow streets
And watched the smoke that rises from the pipes
Of lonely men in shirt-sleeves, leaning out of windows? . . .

I should have been a pair of ragged claws
Scuttling across the floors of silent seas.

    .   .   .   .   .

And the afternoon, the evening, sleeps so peacefully!
Smoothed by long fingers,
Asleep . . . tired . . . or it malingers,
Stretched on the floor, here beside you and me.
Should I, after tea and cakes and ices,
Have the strength to force the moment to its crisis?
But though I have wept and fasted, wept and prayed,
Though I have seen my head (grown slightly bald) brought in upon a platter
I am no prophet—and here's no great matter;
I have seen the moment of my greatness flicker,
And I have seen the eternal Footman hold my coat, and snicker,
And in short, I was afraid.

And would it have been worth it, after all,
After the cups, the marmalade, the tea,
Among the porcelain, among some talk of you and me,
Would it have been worth while,
To have bitten off the matter with a smile,
To have squeezed the universe into a ball
To roll it toward some overwhelming question,
To say: "I am Lazarus, come from the dead,

[697]

Come back to tell you all, I shall tell you all"—
If one, settling a pillow by her head,
 Should say: "That is not what I meant at all.
 That is not it, at all."

And would it have been worth it, after all,
Would it have been worth while,
After the sunsets and the dooryards and the sprinkled streets,
After the novels, after the teacups, after the skirts that trail along the floor—
And this, and so much more?—
It is impossible to say just what I mean!
But as if a magic lantern threw the nerves in patterns on a screen:
Would it have been worth while
If one, settling a pillow or throwing off a shawl,
And turning toward the window, should say:
 "That is not it at all,
 That is not what I meant, at all."

 . . . .

No! I am not Prince Hamlet, nor was meant to be;
Am an attendant lord, one that will do
To swell a progress, start a scene or two,
Advise the prince; no doubt, an easy tool,
Deferential, glad to be of use,
Politic, cautious, and meticulous;
Full of high sentence, but a bit obtuse;
At times, indeed, almost ridiculous—
Almost, at times, the Fool.

I grow old . . . I grow old . . .
I shall wear the bottoms of my trousers rolled.

Shall I part my hair behind? Do I dare to eat a peach?
I shall wear white flannel trousers, and walk upon the beach.
I have heard the mermaids singing, each to each.

I do not think that they will sing to me.

I have seen them riding seaward on the waves
Combing the white hair of the waves blown back
When the wind blows the water white and black.

We have lingered in the chambers of the sea
By sea-girls wreathed with seaweed red and brown
Till human voices wake us, and we drown.

"*Promise you'll wait for me. I want something real to come back to.*"

PORTRAIT OF A LADY

by T. S. Eliot

> Thou hast committed—
> Fornication: but that was in another country,
> And besides, the wench is dead.
> —*The Jew of Malta.*

I

Among the smoke and fog of a December
  afternoon
You have the scene arrange itself—as it
  will seem to do—
With "I have saved this afternoon for
  you";
And four wax candles in the darkened
  room,
Four rings of light upon the ceiling over-
  head,
An atmosphere of Juliet's tomb
Prepared for all the things to be said, or
  left unsaid.
We have been, let us say, to hear the latest
  Pole
Transmit the Preludes, through his hair
  and finger-tips.
"So intimate, this Chopin, that I think his
  soul
Should be resurrected only among friends
Some two or three, who will not touch
  the bloom
That is rubbed and questioned in the con-
  cert room."
—And so the conversation slips
Among velleities and carefully caught re-
  grets
Through attenuated tones of violins
Mingled with remote cornets
And begins.
"You do not know how much they mean
  to me, my friends,
And how, how rare and strange it is, to
  find
In a life composed so much, so much of
  odds and ends,
(For indeed I do not love it . . . you
  knew? you are not blind!
How keen you are!)
To find a friend who has these qualities,
Who has, and gives
Those qualities upon which friendship
  lives.
How much it means that I say this to
  you—
Without these friendships—life, what
  cauchemar!"

Among the windings of the violins
And the ariettes
Of cracked cornets
Inside my brain a dull tom-tom begins
Absurdly hammering a prelude of its own,
Capricious monotone
That is at least one definite "false note."
—Let us take the air, in a tobacco trance,
Admire the monuments,
Discuss the late events,
Correct our watches by the public clocks.
Then sit for half an hour and drink our
  bocks.

II

Now that lilacs are in bloom
She has a bowl of lilacs in her room
And twists one in her fingers while she
  talks.
"Ah, my friend, you do not know, you
  do not know
What life is, you who hold it in your
  hands";

Portrait of a Lady

(Slowly twisting the lilac stalks)
"You let it flow from you, you let it flow,
And youth is cruel, and has no remorse
And smiles at situations which it cannot
 see."
I smile, of course,
And go on drinking tea.
"Yet with these April sunsets, that some-
 how recall
My buried life, and Paris in the Spring,
I feel immeasurably at peace, and find the
 world
To be wonderful and youthful, after all."

The voice returns like the insistent out-of-
 tune
Of a broken violin on an August after-
 noon:
"I am always sure that you understand
My feelings, always sure that you feel,
Sure that across the gulf you reach your
 hand.

You are invulnerable, you have no
 Achilles' heel.
You will go on, and when you have pre-
 vailed
You can say: at this point many a one has
 failed.
But what have I, but what have I, my
 friend,
To give you, what can you receive from
 me?
Only the friendship and the sympathy
Of one about to reach her journey's end.

I shall sit here, serving tea to friends. . . ."

I take my hat: how can I make a cow-
 ardly amends
For what she has said to me?
You will see me any morning in the park
Reading the comics and the sporting page.
Particularly I remark

An English countess goes upon the stage.
A Greek was murdered at a Polish dance,
Another bank defaulter has confessed.
I keep my countenance,
I remain self-possessed
Except when a street piano, mechanical
 and tired
Reiterates some worn-out common song
With the smell of hyacinths across the
 garden
Recalling things that other people have
 desired.
Are these ideas right or wrong?

III

The October night comes down; return-
 ing as before
Except for a slight sensation of being ill
 at ease
I mount the stairs and turn the handle
 of the door
And feel as if I had mounted on my
 hands and knees.

"And so you are going abroad; and when
 do you return?
But that's a useless question.
You hardly know when you are coming
 back,
You will find so much to learn."
My smile falls heavily among the bric-à-
 brac.

"Perhaps you can write to me."
My self-possession flares up for a second;
This is as I had reckoned.
"I have been wondering frequently of late
(But our beginnings never know our
 ends!)
Why we have not developed into friends."
I feel like one who smiles, and turning
 shall remark
Suddenly, his expression in a glass.

[701]

My self-possession gutters; we are really in the dark.

"For everybody said so, all our friends,
They all were sure our feelings would relate
So closely! I myself can hardly understand.
We must leave it now to fate.
You will write, at any rate.
Perhaps it is not too late.
I shall sit here, serving tea to friends."

And I must borrow every changing shape
To find expression . . . dance, dance
Like a dancing bear,
Cry like a parrot, chatter like an ape.
Let us take the air, in a tobacco trance—

Well! and what if she should die some afternoon,
Afternoon gray and smoky, evening yellow and rose;
Should die and leave me sitting pen in hand
With the smoke coming down above the housetops;
Doubtful, for a while
Not knowing what to feel or if I understand
Or whether wise or foolish, tardy or too soon . . .
Would she not have the advantage, after all?
This music is successful with a "dying fall"
Now that we talk of dying—
And should I have the right to smile?

THE HOLLOW MEN

by T. S. ELIOT

A penny for the Old Guy.

MISTAH KURTZ—HE DEAD.

I

We are the hollow men
We are the stuffed men
Leaning together
Headpiece filled with straw. Alas!
Our dried voices, when
We whisper together
Are quiet and meaningless
As wind in dry grass
Or rats' feet over broken glass
In our dry cellar

Shape without form, shade without colour,
Paralysed force, gesture without motion;

Those who have crossed
With direct eyes, to death's other Kingdom
Remember us—if at all—not as lost
Violent souls, but only
As the hollow men
The stuffed men.

II

Eyes I dare not meet in dreams
In death's dream kingdom
These do not appear:
There, the eyes are
Sunlight on a broken column
There, is a tree swinging
And voices are
In the wind's singing

More distant and more solemn
Than a fading star.

Let me be no nearer
In death's dream kingdom
Let me also wear
Such deliberate disguises
Rat's skin, crowskin, crossed staves
In a field
Behaving as the wind behaves
No nearer—

Not that final meeting
In the twilight kingdom

III

This is the dead land
This is cactus land
Here the stone images
Are raised, here they receive
The supplication of a dead man's hand
Under the twinkle of a fading star.

Is it like this
In death's other kingdom
Waking alone
At the hour when we are
Trembling with tenderness
Lips that would kiss
Form prayers to broken stone.

IV

The eyes are not here
There are no eyes here
In this valley of dying stars
In this hollow valley
This broken jaw of our lost kingdoms

In this last of meeting places
We grope together
And avoid speech
Gathered on this beach of the tumid river

Sightless, unless
The eyes reappear
As the perpetual star
Multifoliate rose
Of death's twilight kingdom
The hope only
Of empty men.

V

*Here we go round the prickly pear
Prickly pear prickly pear
Here we go round the prickly pear
At five o'clock in the morning.*

Between the idea
And the reality
Between the motion
And the act
Falls the Shadow
　　For Thine is the Kingdom

Between the conception
And the creation
Between the emotion
And the response
Falls the Shadow
　　Life is very long

Between the desire
And the spasm
Between the potency
And the existence
Between the essence
And the descent
Falls the Shadow
　　For Thine is the Kingdom

For Thine is
Life is
For Thine is the

*This is the way the world ends
This is the way the world ends
This is the way the world ends
Not with a bang but a whimper.*

JOURNEY OF THE MAGI

by T. S. Eliot

'A cold coming we had of it,
Just the worst time of the year
For a journey, and such a long journey:
The ways deep and the weather sharp,
The very dead of winter.'
And the camels galled, sore-footed, refractory,
Lying down in the melting snow.
There were times we regretted
The summer palaces on slopes, the terraces,
And the silken girls bringing sherbet.
Then the camel men cursing and grumbling
And running away, and wanting their liquor and women,
And the night-fires going out, and the lack of shelters,
And the cities hostile and the towns unfriendly
And the villages dirty and charging high prices:
A hard time we had of it.
At the end we preferred to travel all night,
Sleeping in snatches,
With the voices singing in our ears, saying
That this was all folly.

Then at dawn we came down to a temperate valley,
Wet, below the snow line, smelling of vegetation;
With a running stream and a water-mill beating the darkness,
And three trees on the low sky,
And an old white horse galloped away in the meadow.
Then we came to a tavern with vine-leaves over the lintel,
Six hands at an open door dicing for pieces of silver,
And feet kicking the empty wine-skins.
But there was no information, and so we continued
And arrived at evening, not a moment too soon
Finding the place; it was (you may say) satisfactory.

All this was a long time ago, I remember,
And I would do it again, but set down
This set down
This: were we led all that way for
Birth or Death? There was a Birth, certainly,
We had evidence and no doubt. I had seen birth and death,

But had thought they were different; this Birth was
Hard and bitter agony for us, like Death, our death.
We returned to our places, these Kingdoms,
But no longer at ease here, in the old dispensation,
With an alien people clutching their gods.
I should be glad of another death.

TRIUMPHAL MARCH

by T. S. ELIOT

Stone, bronze, stone, steel, stone, oakleaves horses' heels
Over the paving.
And the flags. And the trumpets. And so many eagles.
How many? Count them. And such a press of people.
We hardly knew ourselves that day, or knew the City.
This is the way to the temple, and we so many crowding the way.
So many waiting, how many waiting? what did it matter, on such a day?
Are they coming? No, not yet. You can see some eagles. And hear the trumpets.
Here they come. Is he coming?
The natural wakeful life of our Ego is a perceiving.
We can wait with our stools and our sausages.
What comes first? Can you see? Tell us. It is

	5,800,000	rifles and carbines,
	102,000	machine guns,
	28,000	trench mortars,
	53,000	field and heavy guns,

I cannot tell how many projectiles, mines and fuses,

	13,000	aeroplanes,
	24,000	aeroplane engines,
	50,000	ammunition waggons,
now	55,000	army waggons,
	11,000	field kitchens,
	1,150	field bakeries.

What a time that took. Will it be he now? No,
Those are the golf club Captains, these the Scouts,
And now the *société gymnastique de Poissy*
And now come the Mayor and the Liverymen. Look
There he is now, look:
There is no interrogation in his eyes
Or in the hands, quiet over the horse's neck,
And the eyes watchful, waiting, perceiving, indifferent.

O hidden under the dove's wing, hidden in the turtle's breast,
Under the palmtree at noon, under the running water
At the still point of the turning world. O hidden.

Now they go up to the temple. Then the sacrifice.
Now come the virgins bearing urns, urns containing
Dust
Dust
Dust of dust, and now
Stone, bronze, stone, steel, stone, oakleaves, horses' heels
Over the paving.

That is all we could see. But how many eagles! and how many trumpets!
(And Easter Day, we didn't get to the country,
So we took young Cyril to church. And they rang a bell
And he said right out loud, *crumpets*.)
              Don't throw away that sausage,
It'll come in handy. He's artful. Please, will you
Give us a light?
Light
Light
Et les soldats faisaient la haie? ILS LA FAISAIENT.

EAST COKER

by T. S. ELIOT

I

In my beginning is my end. In succession
Houses rise and fall, crumble, are extended,
Are removed, destroyed, restored, or in their place
Is an open field, or a factory, or a by-pass.
Old stone to new building, old timber to new fires,
Old fires to ashes, and ashes to the earth,
Which is already flesh, fur and faeces,
Bone of man and beast, cornstalk and leaf.
Houses live and die: there is a time for building
And a time for living and for generation
And a time for the wind to break the loosened pane.
And to shake the wainscot where the field-mouse trots
And to shake the tattered arras woven with a silent motto.

East Coker

In my beginning is my end. Now the light falls
Across the open field, leaving the deep lane
Shuttered with branches, dark in the afternoon,
Where you lean against a bank while a van passes,
And the deep lane insists on the direction
Into the village, in the electric heat
Hypnotised. In a warm haze the sultry light
Is absorbed, not refracted, by grey stone.
The dahlias sleep in the empty silence.
Wait for the early owl.
                In that open field
If you do not come too close, if you do not come too close,
On a Summer midnight, you can hear the music
Of the weak pipe and the little drum
And see them dancing around the bonfire
The association of man and woman
In daunsinge, signifying matrimonie—
A dignified and commodious sacrament.
Two and two, necessarye coniunction,
Holding eche other by the hand or the arm
Whiche betokeneth concorde. Round and round the fire
Leaping through the flames, or joined in circles,
Rustically solemn or in rustic laughter
Lifting heavy feet in clumsy shoes,
Earth feet, loam feet, lifted in country mirth
Mirth of those long since under earth
Nourishing the corn. Keeping time,
Keeping the rhythm in their dancing
As in their living in the living seasons
The time of the seasons and the constellations
The time of milking and the time of harvest
The time of the coupling of man and woman
And that of beasts. Feet rising and falling.
Eating and drinking. Dung and death.

Dawn points, and another day
Prepares for heat and silence. Out at sea the dawn wind
Wrinkles and slides. I am here
Or there, or elsewhere. In my beginning.

II

What is the late November doing
With the disturbance of the spring
And creatures of the summer heat,
And snowdrops writhing under feet
And hollyhocks that aim too high
Red into grey and tumble down
Late roses filled with early snow?
Thunder rolled by the rolling stars
Simulates triumphal cars
Deployed in constellated wars
Scorpion fights against the Sun
Until the Sun and Moon go down
Comets weep and Leonids fly
Hunt the heavens and the plains
Whirled in a vortex that shall bring
The world to that destructive fire
Which burns before the ice-cap reigns.

That was a way of putting it—not very satisfactory:
A periphrastic study in a worn-out poetical fashion,
Leaving one still with the intolerable wrestle
With words and meanings. The poetry does not matter.
It was not (to start again) what one had expected.
What was to be the value of the long looked forward to,
Long hoped for calm, the autumnal serenity
And the wisdom of age? Had they deceived us
Or deceived themselves, the quiet-voiced elders,
Bequeathing us merely a receipt for deceit?
The serenity only a deliberate hebetude,
The wisdom only the knowledge of dead secrets
Useless in the darkness into which they peered
Or from which they turned their eyes. There is, it seems to us,
At best, only a limited value
In the knowledge derived from experience.
The knowledge imposes a pattern, and falsifies,
For the pattern is new in every moment
And every moment is a new and shocking
Valuation of all we have been. We are only undeceived
Of that which, deceiving, could no longer harm.
In the middle, not only in the middle of the way
But all the way, in a dark wood, in a bramble,

On the edge of a grimpen, where is no secure foothold,
And menaced by monsters, fancy lights,
Risking enchantment. Do not let me hear
Of the wisdom of old men, but rather of their folly,
Their fear of fear and frenzy, their fear of possession,
Of belonging to another, or to others, or to God.
The only wisdom we can hope to acquire
Is the wisdom of humility: humility is endless.

The houses are all gone under the sea.

The dancers are all gone under the hill.

III

O dark dark dark. They all go into the dark,
The vacant interstellar spaces, the vacant into the vacant,
The captains, merchant bankers, eminent men of letters,
The generous patrons of art, the statesmen and the rulers,
Distinguished civil servants, chairmen of many committees,
Industrial lords and petty contractors, all go into the dark,
And dark the Sun and Moon, and the Almanach de Gotha
And the Stock Exchange Gazette, the Directory of Directors,
And cold the sense and lost the motive of action.
And we all go with them, into the silent funeral,
Nobody's funeral, for there is no one to bury.
I said to my soul, be still, and let the dark come upon you
Which shall be the darkness of God. As, in a theatre,
The lights are extinguished, for the scene to be changed
With a hollow rumble of wings, with a movement of darkness on darkness,
And we know that the hills and the trees, the distant panorama
And the bold imposing façade are all being rolled away—
Or as, when an underground train, in the tube, stops too long between stations
And the conversation rises and slowly fades into silence
And you see behind every face the mental emptiness deepen
Leaving only the growing terror of nothing to think about;
Or when, under ether, the mind is conscious but conscious of nothing—
I said to my soul, be still, and wait without hope
For hope would be hope for the wrong thing; wait without love
For love would be love of the wrong thing; there is yet faith
But the faith and the love and the hope are all in the waiting.
Wait without thought, for you are not ready for thought:
So the darkness shall be the light, and the stillness the dancing.

Whisper of running streams, and winter lightning.
The wild thyme unseen and the wild strawberry,
The laughter in the garden, echoed ecstasy
Not lost, but requiring, pointing to the agony
Of death and birth.
                You say I am repeating
Something I have said before. I shall say it again.
Shall I say it again? In order to arrive there,
To arrive where you are, to get from where you are not,
    You must go by a way wherein there is no ecstasy.
In order to arrive at what you do not know
    You must go by a way which is the way of ignorance.
In order to possess what you do not possess
    You must go by the way of dispossession.
In order to arrive at what you are not
    You must go through the way in which you are not.
And what you do not know is the only thing you know
And what you own is what you do not own
And where you are is where you are not.

IV

The wounded surgeon plies the steel
That questions the distempered part;
Beneath the bleeding hands we feel
The sharp compassion of the healer's art
Resolving the enigma of the fever chart.

Our only health is the disease
If we obey the dying nurse
Whose constant care is not to please
But to remind of our, and Adam's curse,
And that, to be restored, our sickness must grow worse.

The whole earth is our hospital
Endowed by the ruined millionaire,
Wherein, if we do well, we shall
Die of the absolute paternal care
That will not leave us, but prevents us everywhere.

The chill ascends from feet to knees,
The fever sings in mental wires.
If to be warmed, then I must freeze

And quake in frigid purgatorial fires
Of which the flame is roses, and the smoke is briars.

The dripping blood our only drink,
The bloody flesh our only food:
In spite of which we like to think
That we are sound, substantial flesh and blood—
Again, in spite of that, we call this Friday good.

v

So here I am, in the middle way, having had twenty years—
Twenty years largely wasted, the years of *l'entre deux guerres*—
Trying to learn to use words, and every attempt
Is a wholly new start, and a different kind of failure
Because one has only learnt to get the better of words
For the thing one no longer has to say, or the way in which
One is no longer disposed to say it. And so each venture
Is a new beginning, a raid on the inarticulate
With shabby equipment always deteriorating
In the general mess of imprecision of feeling,
Undisciplined squads of emotion. And what there is to conquer
By strength and submission, has already been discovered
Once or twice, or several times, by men whom one cannot hope
To emulate—but there is no competition—
There is only the fight to recover what has been lost
And found and lost again and again: but now, under conditions
That seem unpropitious. But perhaps neither gain nor loss.
For us, there is only the trying. The rest is not our business.

Home is where one starts from. As we grow older
The world becomes stranger, the pattern more complicated
Of dead and living. Not the intense moment
Isolated, with no before and after,
But a lifetime burning in every moment
And not the lifetime of one man only
But of old stones that cannot be deciphered.
There is a time for the evening under starlight,
A time for the evening under lamplight
(The evening with the photograph album).
Love is most nearly itself
When here and now cease to matter.
Old men ought to be explorers

[711]

Here and there does not matter
We must be still and still moving
Into another intensity
For a further union, a deeper communion
Through the dark cold and the empty desolation,
The wave cry, the wind cry, the vast waters
Of the petrel and the porpoise. In my end is my beginning.

MACAVITY: THE MYSTERY CAT
by T. S. ELIOT

Macavity's a Mystery Cat: he's called the Hidden Paw—
For he's the master criminal who can defy the Law.
He's the bafflement of Scotland Yard, the Flying Squad's despair:
For when they reach the scene of crime—*Macavity's not there!*

Macavity, Macavity, there's no one like Macavity,
He's broken every human law, he breaks the law of gravity.
His powers of levitation would make a fakir stare,
And when you reach the scene of crime—*Macavity's not there!*
You may seek him in the basement, you may look up in the air—
But I tell you once and once again, *Macavity's not there!*

Macavity's a ginger cat, he's very tall and thin;
You would know him if you saw him, for his eyes are sunken in.
His brow is deeply lined with thought, his head is highly domed;
His coat is dusty from neglect, his whiskers are uncombed.
He sways his head from side to side, with movements like a snake;
And when you think he's half asleep, he's always wide awake.

Macavity, Macavity, there's no one like Macavity,
For he's a fiend in feline shape, a monster of depravity.
You may meet him in a by-street, you may see him in the square—
But when a crime's discovered, then *Macavity's not there!*

He's outwardly respectable. (They say he cheats at cards.)
And his footprints are not found in any file of Scotland Yard's.
And when the larder's looted, or the jewel-case is rifled,
Or when the milk is missing, or another Peke's been stifled,
Or the greenhouse glass is broken, and the trellis past repair—
Ay, there's the wonder of the thing! *Macavity's not there!*

And when the Foreign Office find a Treaty's gone astray,
Or the Admiralty lose some plans and drawings by the way,
There may be a scrap of paper in the hall or on the stair—
But it's useless to investigate—*Macavity's not there!*
And when the loss has been disclosed, the Secret Service say:
"It *must* have been Macavity!"—but he's a mile away.
You'll be sure to find him resting, or a-licking of his thumbs,
Or engaged in doing complicated long division sums.

Macavity, Macavity, there's no one like Macavity,
There never was a Cat of such deceitfulness and suavity.
He always has an alibi, and one or two to spare:
At whatever time the deed took place—MACAVITY WASN'T THERE!
And they say that all the Cats whose wicked deeds are widely known
(I might mention Mungojerrie, I might mention Griddlebone)
Are nothing more than agents for the Cat who all the time
Just controls their operations: the Napoleon of Crime!

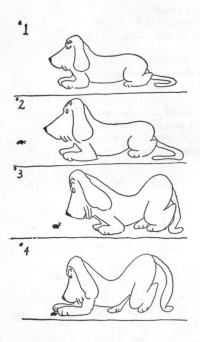

THE BLOODHOUND

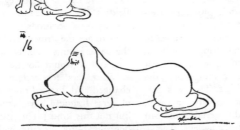

AND THE BUG   Drawing by Thurber, © 1932 *The New Yorker Magazine,* Inc.

from Foreword to THE SELECTED POETRY OF ROBINSON JEFFERS

by ROBINSON JEFFERS

LONG AGO, . . . it became evident to me that poetry—if it was to survive at all—must reclaim some of the power and reality that it was so hastily surrendering to prose. The modern French poetry of that time, and the most "modern" of the English poetry, seemed to me thoroughly defeatist, as if poetry were in terror of prose, and desperately trying to save its soul from the victor by giving up its body. It was becoming slight and fantastic, abstract, unreal, eccentric; and was not even saving its soul, for these are generally anti-poetic qualities. It must reclaim substance and sense, and physical and psychological reality. This feeling has been basic in my mind since then. It led me to write narrative poetry, and to draw subjects from contemporary life; to present aspects of life that modern poetry had generally avoided; and to attempt the expression of philosophic and scientific ideas in verse. It was not in my mind to open new fields for poetry, but only to reclaim old freedom.

Still it was obvious that poetry and prose are different things; their provinces overlap, but must not be confused. Prose, of course, is free of all fields; it seemed to me, reading poetry and trying to write it, that poetry is bound to concern itself chiefly with permanent things and the permanent aspects of life. That was perhaps the great distinction between them, as regards subject and material. Prose can discuss matters of the moment; poetry must deal with things that a reader two thousand years away could understand and be moved by. This excludes much of the circumstance of modern life, especially in the cities. Fashions, forms of machinery, the more complex social, financial, political adjustments, and so forth, are all ephemeral, exceptional; they exist but will never exist again. Poetry must concern itself with (relatively) permanent things. These have poetic value; the ephemeral has only news value.

Another formative principle came to me from a phrase of Nietzsche's: "The poets? The poets lie too much." I was nineteen when the phrase stuck in my mind; a dozen years passed before it worked effectively, and I decided not to tell lies in verse. Not to feign any emotion that I did not feel; not to pretend to believe in optimism or pessimism, or unreversible progress; not to say anything because it was popular, or generally accepted, or fashionable in intellectual circles, unless I myself believed it; and not to believe easily. These negatives limit the field; I am not recommending them but for my own occasions.

Here are the principles that conditioned the verse in this book before it was written; but it would not have been written at all except for certain accidents that changed and directed my life. (Some kind of verse I should have written, of course, but not this kind.) The first of these accidents was my meeting with the woman

:o whom this book is dedicated, and her influence, constant since that time. My nature is cold and undiscriminating; she excited and focused it, gave it eyes and nerves and sympathies. She never saw any of my poems until they were finished and typed, yet by her presence and conversation she has co-authored every one of them. Sometimes I think there must be some value in them, if only for that reason. She is more like a woman in a Scotch ballad, passionate, untamed and rather heroic—or like a falcon—than like any ordinary person.

A second piece of pure accident brought us to the Monterey coast mountains, where for the first time in my life I could see people living—amid magnificent unspoiled scenery—essentially as they did in the Idyls or the Sagas, or in Homer's Ithaca. Here was life purged of its ephemeral accretions. Men were riding after cattle, or plowing the headland, hovered by white sea-gulls, as they have done for thousands of years, and will for thousands of years to come. Here was contemporary life that was also permanent life; and not shut from the modern world but conscious of it and related to it; capable of expressing its spirit, but unencumbered by the mass of poetically irrelevant details and complexities that make a civilization.

By this time I was nearing thirty, and still a whole series of accidents was required to stir my lazy energies to the point of writing verse that seemed to be —whether good or bad—at least my own voice.

HURT HAWKS

by Robinson Jeffers

I

The broken pillar of the wing jags from the clotted shoulder,
The wing trails like a banner in defeat,
No more to use the sky forever but live with famine
And pain a few days: cat nor coyote
Will shorten the week of waiting for death, there is game without talons.
He stands under the oak-bush and waits
The lame feet of salvation; at night he remembers freedom
And flies in a dream, the dawns ruin it.
He is strong and pain is worse to the strong, incapacity is worse.
The curs of the day come and torment him
At distance, no one but death the redeemer will humble that head,
The intrepid readiness, the terrible eyes.
The wild God of the world is sometimes merciful to those
That ask mercy, not often to the arrogant.
You do not know him, you communal people, or you have forgotten him;
Intemperate and savage, the hawk remembers him;
Beautiful and wild, the hawks, and men that are dying, remember him.

II

I'd sooner, except the penalties, kill a man than a hawk; but the great redtail
Had nothing left but unable misery
From the bone too shattered for mending, the wing that trailed under his talons
    when he moved.
We had fed him six weeks, I gave him freedom,
He wandered over the foreland hill and returned in the evening, asking for death,
Not like a beggar, still eyed with the old
Implacable arrogance. I gave him the lead gift in the twilight. What fell was relaxed,
Owl-downy, soft feminine feathers; but what
Soared: the fierce rush: the night-herons by the flooded river cried fear at its rising
Before it was quite unsheathed from reality.

TO THE STONE-CUTTERS

by ROBINSON JEFFERS

Stone-cutters fighting time with marble, you foredefeated
Challengers of oblivion,
Eat cynical earnings, knowing rock splits, records fall down,
The square-limbed Roman letters
Scale in the thaws, wear in the rain. The poet as well
Builds his monument mockingly;
For man will be blotted out, the blithe earth die, the brave sun
Die blind and blacken to the heart:
Yet stones have stood for a thousand years, and pained thoughts found
The honey of peace in old poems.

SHINE, PERISHING REPUBLIC

by ROBINSON JEFFERS

While this America settles in the mould of its vulgarity, heavily thickening to empire,
And protest, only a bubble in the molten mass, pops and sighs out, and the mass
    hardens,

I sadly smiling remember that the flower fades to make fruit, the fruit rots to make
    earth.
Out of the mother; and through the spring exultances, ripeness and decadence; and
    home to the mother.

[7 1 8]

u making haste haste on decay: not blameworthy; life is good, be it stubbornly long or suddenly

. mortal splendor: meteors are not needed less than mountains: shine, perishing republic.

But for my children, I would have them keep their distance from the thickening center; corruption
Never has been compulsory, when the cities lie at the monster's feet there are left the mountains.

And boys, be in nothing so moderate as in love of man, a clever servant, insufferable master.
There is the trap that catches noblest spirits, that caught—they say—God, when he walked on earth.

THE PURSE-SEINE

by ROBINSON JEFFERS

Our sardine fishermen work at night in the dark of the moon; daylight or moonlight
They could not tell where to spread the net, unable to see the phosphorescence of the shoals of fish.
They work northward from Monterey, coasting Santa Cruz; off New Year's Point or off Pigeon Point
The look-out man will see some lakes of milk-color light on the sea's night-purple; he points, and the helmsman
Turns the dark prow, the motorboat circles the gleaming shoal and drifts out her seine-net. They close the circle
And purse the bottom of the net, then with great labor haul it in.

I cannot tell you
How beautiful the scene is, and a little terrible, then, when the crowded fish
Know they are caught, and wildly beat from one wall to the other of their closing destiny the phosphorescent
Water to a pool of flame, each beautiful slender body sheeted with flame, like a live rocket
A comet's tail wake of clear yellow flame; while outside the narrowing
Floats and cordage of the net great sea-lions come up to watch, sighing in the dark; the vast walls of night
Stand erect to the stars.

Lately I was looking from a night mountain-top
On a wide city, the colored splendor, galaxies of light: how could I help but rec
    the seine-net
Gathering the luminous fish? I cannot tell you how beautiful the city appeared
    and a little terrible.
I thought, We have geared the machines and locked all together into interdepend-
    ence; we have built the great cities; now
There is no escape. We have gathered vast populations incapable of free survival,
    insulated
From the strong earth, each person in himself helpless, on all dependent. The circle
    is closed, and the net
Is being hauled in. They hardly feel the cords drawing, yet they shine already. The
    inevitable mass-disasters
Will not come in our time nor in our children's, but we and our children
Must watch the net draw narrower, government take all powers—or revolution,
    and the new government
Take more than all, add to kept bodies kept souls—or anarchy, the mass-disasters.

These things are Progress;
Do you marvel our verse is troubled or frowning, while it keeps its reason? Or it
    lets go, lets the mood flow
In the manner of the recent young men into mere hysteria, splintered gleams,
    crackled laughter. But they are quite wrong.
There is no reason for amazement: surely one always knew that cultures decay, and
    life's end is death.

THE ANSWER

by ROBINSON JEFFERS

Then what is the answer?—Not to be deluded by dreams.
To know that great civilizations have broken down into violence, and their tyrants
    come, many times before.
When open violence appears, to avoid it with honor or choose the least ugly faction;
    these evils are essential.
To keep one's own integrity, be merciful and uncorrupted and not wish for evil;
    and not be duped
By dreams of universal justice or happiness. These dreams will not be fulfilled.
To know this, and know that however ugly the parts appear the whole remains
    beautiful. A severed hand
Is an ugly thing, and man dissevered from the earth and stars and his history . . .
    for contemplation or in fact . . .

:n appears atrociously ugly. Integrity is wholeness, the greatest beauty is

ganic wholeness, the wholeness of life and things, the divine beauty of the uni-
verse. Love that, not man

part from that, or else you will share man's pitiful confusions, or drown in despair
when his days darken.

THE INQUISITORS

by Robinson Jeffers

Coming around a corner of the dark trail . . . what was wrong with the valley?

Azevedo checked his horse and sat staring: it was all changed. It was occupied. There
were three hills

Where none had been: and firelight flickered red on their knees between them: if
they were hills:

They were more like Red Indians around a camp-fire, grave and dark, mountain-
high, hams on heels

Squatting around a little fire of hundred-foot logs. Azevedo remembers he felt an
ice-brook

Glide on his spine; he slipped down from the saddle and hid

In the brush by the trail, above the black redwood forest. This was the Little Sur
South Fork,

Its forest valley; the man had come in at nightfall over Bowcher's Gap, and a high
moon hunted

Through running clouds. He heard the rumble of a voice, heavy not loud, saying,
"I gathered some,

You can inspect them." One of the hills moved a huge hand

And poured its contents on a table-topped rock that stood in the firelight; men and
women fell out;

Some crawled and some lay quiet; the hills leaned to eye them. One said: "It seems
hardly possible

Such fragile creatures could be so noxious." Another answered,

"True, but we've seen. But it is only recently they have the power." The third
answered, "That bomb?"

"Oh," he said, "—and the rest." He reached across and picked up one of the mites
from the rock, and held it

Close to his eyes, and very carefully with finger and thumbnail peeled it: by chance
a young female

With long black hair: it was too helpless even to scream. He held it by one white
  leg and stared at it:
"I can see nothing strange: only so fragile." The third hill answered, "We suppose
  it is something
Inside the head." Then the other split the skull with his thumbnail, squinting his
  eyes and peering, and said,
"A drop of marrow. How could that spoil the earth?" "Nevertheless," he answered,
"They have that bomb. The blasts and the fires are nothing: freckles on the earth:
  the emanations
Might set the whole planet into a tricky fever
And destroy much." "Themselves," he answered. "Let them. Why not?" "No," he
  answered, "life."

Azevedo

Still watched in horror, and all three of the hills
Picked little animals from the rock, peeled them and cracked them, or toasted them
On the red coals, or split their bodies from the crotch upward
To stare inside. They said, "It remains a mystery. However," they said,
"It is not likely they can destroy all life: the planet is capacious. Life would surely
  grow up again
From grubs in the soil, or the newt and toad level, and be beautiful again. And
  again perhaps break its legs
On its own cleverness: who can forecast the future?" The speaker yawned, and with
  his flat hand
Brushed the rock clean; the three slowly stood up,
Taller than Pico Blanco into the sky, their Indian-beaked heads in the moon-cloud,
And trampled their watchfire out and went away southward, stepping across the
  Ventana mountains.

YOU, ANDREW MARVELL

by ARCHIBALD MACLEISH

And here face down beneath the sun
And here upon earth's noonward height
To feel the always coming on
The always rising of the night

To feel creep up the curving east
The earthy chill of dusk and slow
Upon those under lands the vast
And ever climbing shadow grow

And strange at Ecbatan the trees
Take leaf by leaf the evening strange
The flooding dark about their knees
The mountains over Persia change

And now at Kermanshah the gate
Dark empty and the withered grass
And through the twilight now the late
Few travelers in the westward pass

And Baghdad darken and the bridge
Across the silent river gone

And through Arabia the edge
Of evening widen and steal on

And deepen on Palmyra's street
The wheel rut in the ruined stone
And Lebanon fade out and Crete
High through the clouds and overblown

And over Sicily the air
Still flashing with the landward gulls
And loom and slowly disappear
The sails above the shadowy hulls

And Spain go under and the shore
Of Africa the gilded sand
And evening vanish and no more
The low pale light across that land

Nor now the long light on the sea

And here face downward in the sun
To feel how swift how secretly
The shadow of the night comes on . . .

from THE HAMLET OF A. MACLEISH

by ARCHIBALD MACLEISH

Night after night I lie like this listening.
Night after night I cannot sleep. I wake
Knowing something, thinking something has happened.
I have this feeling a great deal. I have
Sadness often. At night I have this feeling.
Waking I feel this pain as though I knew
Something not to be thought of, something unbearable.
I feel this pain at night as though some
Terrible thing had happened. At night the sky
Opens, the near things vanish, the bright walls
Fall, and the stars were always there, and the dark

The selections from Archibald MacLeish's *Poems 1924-1933* are used by permission of the publishers, Houghton Mifflin Company.

There and the cold and the stillness. I wake and stand
A long time by the window. I always think
The trees know the way they are silent. I always
Think some one has spoken, some one has told me.
Reading the books I always think so, reading
Words overheard in the books, reading the words
Like words in a strange language. I always hear
Music like that. I almost remember with music . . .
This is not what you think. It is not that. I swim
Every day at the beach under the fig tree.
I swim very well and far out. The smell
Of pine comes over the water. The wind blurs
Seaward. And afternoons I walk to the phare.
Much of the time I do not think anything;
Much of the time I do not even notice.
And then, speaking, closing a door, I see
Strangely as though I almost saw now, some
Shape of things I have always seen, the sun
White on a house and the windows open and swallows
In and out of the wallpaper, the moon's face
Faint by day in a mirror; I see some
Changed thing that is telling, something that almost
Tells—and this pain then, then this pain. And no
Words, only these shapes of things that seem
Ways of knowing what it is I am knowing.
I write these things in books, on pieces of paper.
I have written 'The wind rises . . .' I have written 'Bells
Plunged in the wind . . .' I have written 'Like
Doors . . .' 'Like evening . . .'
It is always the same: I cannot read what the words say.
It is always the same: there are signs and I cannot read them.
There are empty streets and the blinds drawn and the sky
Sliding in windows. There are lights before
Dawn in the yellow transoms over the doors.
There are steps that pass and pass all night that are always
One, always the same step passing . . .
I have traveled a great deal. I have seen at Homs
The cranes over the river and Isfahan
The fallen tiles in the empty garden, and Shiraz
Far off, the cypresses under the hill.
It is always the same. I have seen on the Kazvin road
On the moon grey desert the leafless wind,
The wind raging in moon-dusk. Or the light that comes
Seaward with slow oars from the mouth of the Euphrates.

American Letter

I have heard the nightingales in the thickets of Gilan,
And at dawn, at Teheran, I have heard from the ancient
Westward greying face of the wandering planet
The voices calling the small new name of god,
The voices answered with cockcrow, answered at dusk
With the cry of jackals far away in the gardens.
I have heard the name of the moon beyond those mountains.
It is always the same. It is always as though some
Smell of leaves had made me not quite remember;
As though I had turned to look and there were no one.
It has always been secret like that with me.
Always something has not been said. Always
The stones were there, the trees were there, the motionless
Hills have appeared in the dusk to me, the moon
Has stood a long time white and still in the window.
Always the earth has been turned away from me hiding
The veiled eyes and the wind in the leaves has not spoken . . .

As now the night is still. As the night now
Stands at the farthest off of touch and like
A raised hand held upon the empty air
Means and is silent.
                    Look! It waves me still . . .
    I say Go on! Go on!

                         As the whole night now
Made visible behind this darkness seems
To beckon to me . . .

AMERICAN LETTER

for Gerald Murphy

by ARCHIBALD MACLEISH

The wind is east but the hot weather continues,
Blue and no clouds, the sound of the leaves thin,
Dry like the rustling of paper, scored across
With the slate-shrill screech of the locusts.
                              The tossing of
Pines is the low sound. In the wind's running
The wild carrots smell of the burning sun.
Why should I think of the dolphins at Capo di Mele?

[725]

Why should I see in my mind the taut sail
And the hill over St.-Tropez and your hand on the tiller?
Why should my heart be troubled with palms still?
I am neither a sold boy nor a Chinese official
Sent to sicken in Pa for some Lo-Yang dish.
This is my own land, my sky, my mountain:
This—not the humming pines and the surf and the sound
At the Ferme Blanche, nor Port Cros in the dusk and the harbor
Floating the motionless ship and the sea-drowned star.
I am neither Po Chü-i nor another after
Far from home, in a strange land, daft
For the talk of his own sort and the taste of his lettuces.
This land is my native land. And yet
I am sick for home for the red roofs and the olives,
And the foreign words and the smell of the sea fall.
How can a wise man have two countries?
How can a man have the earth and the wind and want
A land far off, alien, smelling of palm-trees
And the yellow gorse at noon in the long calms?

It is a strange thing—to be an American.
Neither an old house it is with the air
Tasting of hung herbs and the sun returning
Year after year to the same door and the churn
Making the same sound in the cool of the kitchen
Mother to son's wife, and the place to sit
Marked in the dusk by the worn stone at the wellhead—
That—nor the eyes like each other's eyes and the skull
Shaped to the same fault and the hands' sameness.
Neither a place it is nor a blood name.
America is West and the wind blowing.
America is a great word and the snow,
A way, a white bird, the rain falling,
A shining thing in the mind and the gulls' call.
America is neither a land nor a people,
A word's shape it is, a wind's sweep—
America is alone: many together,
Many of one mouth, of one breath,
Dressed as one—and none brothers among them:
Only the taught speech and the aped tongue.
America is alone and the gulls calling.

It is a strange thing to be an American.
It is strange to live on the high world in the stare
Of the naked sun and the stars as our bones live.
Men in the old lands housed by their rivers.

They built their towns in the vales in the earth's shelter.
We first inhabit the world. We dwell
On the half earth, on the open curve of a continent.
Sea is divided from sea by the day-fall. The dawn
Rides the low east with us many hours;
First are the capes, then are the shorelands, now
The blue Appalachians faint at the day rise;
The willows shudder with light on the long Ohio:
The Lakes scatter the low sun: the prairies
Slide out of dark: in the eddy of clean air
The smoke goes up from the high plains of Wyoming:
The steep Sierras arise: the struck foam
Flames at the wind's heel on the far Pacific.
Already the noon leans to the eastern cliff:
The elms darken the door and the dust-heavy lilacs.

It is strange to sleep in the bare stars and to die
On an open land where few bury before us:
(From the new earth the dead return no more.)
It is strange to be born of no race and no people.
In the old lands they are many together. They keep
The wise past and the words spoken in common.
They remember the dead with their hands, their mouths dumb.
They answer each other with two words in their meeting.
They live together in small things. They eat
The same dish, their drink is the same and their proverbs.
Their youth is like. They are like in their ways of love.
They are many men. There are always others beside them.
Here it is one man and another and wide
On the darkening hills the faint smoke of the houses.
Here it is one man and the wind in the boughs.

Therefore our hearts are sick for the south water.
The smell of the gorse comes back to our night thought.
We are sick at heart for the red roofs and the olives;
We are sick at heart for the voice and the footfall. . .

Therefore we will not go though the sea call us.

This, this is our land, this is our people,
This that is neither a land nor a race. We must reap
The wind here in the grass for our soul's harvest:
Here we must eat our salt or our bones starve.
Here we must live or live only as shadows.
This is our race, we that have none, that have had
Neither the old walls nor the voices around us,

This is our land, this is our ancient ground—
The raw earth, the mixed bloods and the strangers,
The different eyes, the wind, and the heart's change.
These we will not leave though the old call us.
This is our country-earth, our blood, our kind.
Here we will live our years till the earth blind us—
The wind blows from the east. The leaves fall.
Far off in the pines a jay rises.
The wind smells of haze and the wild ripe apples.

I think of the masts at Cette and the sweet rain.

MEN

(*On a phrase of Apollinaire*)

by Archibald MacLeish

Our history is grave noble and tragic
We trusted the look of the sun on the green leaves
We built our towns of stone with enduring ornaments
We worked the hard flint for basins of water

We believed in the feel of the earth under us
We planted corn grapes apple-trees rhubarb
Nevertheless we knew others had died
Everything we have done has been faithful and dangerous

We believed in the promises made by the brows of women
We begot children at night in the warm wool
We comforted those who wept in fear on our shoulders
Those who comforted us had themselves vanished

We fought at the dikes in the bright sun for the pride of it
We beat drums and marched with music and laughter
We were drunk and lay with our fine dreams in the straw
We saw the stars through the hair of lewd women

Our history is grave noble and tragic
Many of us have died and are not remembered
Many cities are gone and their channels broken
We have lived a long time in this land and with honor

The selection from Archibald MacLeish's *Poems 1924-1933* is used by permission of the publishers, Houghton Mifflin Company.

SPEECH TO THOSE WHO SAY COMRADE
by ARCHIBALD MACLEISH

The brotherhood is not by the blood certainly:
But neither are men brothers by speech—by saying so:
Men are brothers by life lived and are hurt for it:

Hunger and hurt are the great begetters of brotherhood:
Humiliation has gotten much love:
Danger I say is the nobler father and mother:

Those are as brothers whose bodies have shared fear
Or shared harm or shared hurt or indignity.
Why are the old soldiers brothers and nearest?

For this: with their minds they go over the sea a little
And find themselves in their youth again as they were in
Soissons and Meaux and at Ypres and those cities:

A French loaf and the girls with their eyelids painted
Bring back to aging and lonely men
Their twentieth year and the metal odor of danger:

It is this in life which of all things is tenderest—
To remember together with the unknown men the days
Common also to them and perils ended:

It is this which makes of many a generation—
A wave of men who having the same years
Have in common the same dead and the changes.

The solitary and unshared experience
Dies of itself like the violations of love
Or lives on as the dead live eerily.

The unshared and single man must cover his
Loneliness as a girl her shame for the way of
Life is neither by one man nor by suffering.

Who are the born brothers in truth? The puddlers
Scorched by the same flame in the same foundries:
Those who have spit on the same boards with the blood in it:

Ridden the same rivers with green logs:
Fought the police in the parks of the same cities:
Grinned for the same blows: the same flogging:

Veterans out of the same ships—factories—
Expeditions for fame: the founders of continents:
Those that hid in Geneva a time back:

Those that have hidden and hunted and all such—
Fought together: labored together: they carry the
Common look like a card and they pass touching.

Brotherhood! No word said can make you brothers!
Brotherhood only the brave earn and by danger or
Harm or by bearing hurt and by no other

Brotherhood here in the strange world is the rich and
Rarest giving of life and the most valued:
Not to be had for a word or a week's wishing.

AMERICA WAS PROMISES

by ARCHIBALD MacLEISH

Who is the voyager in these leaves?
Who is the traveler in this journey
Deciphers the revolving night: receives
The signal from the light returning?

America was promises to whom?

                        East were the
Dead kings and the remembered sepulchres:
West was the grass.
                        The groves of the oaks were at evening.

Eastward are the nights where we have slept.

And we move on: we move down:
With the first light we push forward:
We descend from the past as a wandering people from mountains.
We cross into the day to be discovered.
The dead are left where they fall—at dark
At night late under the coverlets.

Archibald MacLeish, *America Was Promises*. Reprinted by permission of the publishers, Duell, Sloan & Pearce, Inc.

America Was Promises

We mark the place with the shape of our teeth on our fingers.
The room is left as it was: the love

Who is the traveler in these leaves these
Annual waters and beside the doors
Jonquils: then the rose: the eaves
Heaping the thunder up: the mornings
Opening on like great valleys
Never till now approached: the familiar trees
Far off: distant with the future:
The hollyhocks beyond the afternoons:
The butterflies over the ripening fruit on the balconies:
And all beautiful
All before us

America was always promises.
From the first voyage and the first ship there were promises—
'the tropic bird which does not sleep at sea'
'the great mass of dark heavy clouds which is a sign'
'the drizzle of rain without wind which is a sure sign'
'the whale which is an indication'
'the stick appearing to be carved with iron'
'the stalk loaded with roseberries'
'and all these signs were from the west'
'and all night heard birds passing.'

Who is the voyager on these coasts?
Who is the traveler in these waters
Expects the future as a shore: foresees
Like Indies to the west the ending—he
The rumor of the surf intends?

America was promises—to whom?

Jefferson knew:
Declared it before God and before history:
Declares it still in the remembering tomb.
The promises were Man's: the land was his—
Man endowed by his Creator:
Earnest in love: perfectible by reason:
Just and perceiving justice: his natural nature
Clear and sweet at the source as springs in trees are.
It was Man the promise contemplated.
The times had chosen Man: no other:

Bloom on his face of every future:
Brother of stars and of all travelers:
Brother of time and of all mysteries:
Brother of grass also: of fruit trees.
It was Man who had been promised: who should have.
Man was to ride from the Tidewater: over the Gap:
West and South with the water: taking the book with him:
Taking the wheat seed: corn seed: pip of apple:
Building liberty a farmyard wide
Breeding for useful labor: for good looks:
For husbandry: humanity: for pride—
Practising self-respect and common decency.

And Man turned into men in Philadelphia
Practising prudence on a long-term lease:
Building liberty to fit the parlor:
Bred for crystal on the frontroom shelves:
Just and perceiving justice by the dollar:
Patriotic with the bonds at par
(And their children's children brag of their deeds for the Colonies).
Man rode up from the Tidewater: over the Gap:
Turned into men: turned into two-day settlers:
Lawyers with the land-grants in their caps:
Coon-skin voters wanting theirs and getting it.

Turned the promises to capital: invested it.

America was always promises:
'the wheel like a sun as big as a cart wheel
     with many sorts of pictures on it
     the whole of fine gold'

'twenty golden ducks
     beautifully worked and very natural looking
     and some like dogs of the kind they keep'

And they waved us west from the dunes: they cried out
Colua! Colua!
Mexico! Mexico! . . . Colua!

America was promises to whom?

Old Man Adams knew. He told us—
An aristocracy of compound interest
Hereditary through the common stock!
We'd have one sure before the mare was older.
"The first want of every man was his dinner:

The second his girl." Kings were by the pocket.
Wealth made blood made wealth made blood made wealthy.
Enlightened selfishness gave lasting light.
Winners bred grandsons: losers only bred!

And the Aristocracy of politic selfishness
Bought the land up: bought the towns: the sites:
The goods: the government: the people. Bled them.
Sold them. Kept the profit. Lost itself.

The Aristocracy of Wealth and Talents
Turned its talents into wealth and lost them.
Turned enlightened selfishness to wealth.
Turned self-interest into bankbooks: balanced them.
Bred out: bred to fools: to hostlers:
Card sharps: well dressed women: dancefloor doublers.
The Aristocracy of Wealth and Talents
Sold its talents: bought the public notice:
Drank in public: went to bed in public:
Patronized the arts in public: pall'd with
Public authors public beauties: posed in
Public postures for the public page.
The Aristocracy of Wealth and Talents
Withered of talent and ashamed of wealth
Bred to sonsinlaw: insane relations:
Girls with open secrets: sailors' Galahads:
Prurient virgins with the tales to tell:
Women with dead wombs and living wishes.

The Aristocracy of Wealth and Talents
Moved out: settled on the Continent:
Sat beside the water at Rapallo:
Died in a rented house: unwept: unhonored.

And the child says I see the lightning on you.

The weed between the railroad tracks
Tasting of sweat: tasting of poverty:
The bitter and pure taste where the hawk hovers:
Native as the deer bone in the sand

O my America for whom?

For whom the promises? For whom the river
"It flows west! Look at the ripple of it!"

[733]

The grass "So that it was wonderful to see
And endless without end with wind wonderful!"
The Great Lakes: landless as oceans: their beaches
Coarse sand: clean gravel: pebbles:
Their bluffs smelling of sunflowers: smelling of surf:
Of fresh water: of wild sunflowers . . . wilderness.
For whom the evening mountains on the sky:
The night wind from the west: the moon descending?

Tom Paine knew.
Tom Paine knew the People.
The promises were spoken to the People.
History was voyages toward the People.
Americas were landfalls of the People.
Stars and expectations were the signals of the People.

Whatever was truly built the People had built it.
Whatever was taken down they had taken down.
Whatever was worn they had worn—ax-handles: fiddle-bows:
Sills of doorways: names for children: for mountains.
Whatever was long forgotten they had forgotten—
Fame of the great: names of the rich and their mottos.
The People had the promises: they'd keep them.
They waited their time in the world: they had wise sayings.
They counted out their time by day to day.
They counted it out day after day into history.
They had time and to spare in the spill of their big fists.
They had all the time there was like a handful of wheat seed.
When the time came they would speak and the rest would listen.

And the time came and the People did not speak.

The time came: the time comes: the speakers
Come and these who speak are not the People.

These who speak with gunstocks at the doors:
These the coarse ambitious priest
Leads by the bloody fingers forward:
These who reach with stiffened arm to touch
What none who took dared touch before:
These who touch the truth are not the People.

These the savage fables of the time
Lick at the fingers as a bitch will waked at morning:
These who teach the lie are not the People.

The time came: the time comes

America Was Promises

Comes and to whom? To these? Was it for these
The surf was secret on the new-found shore?
Was it for these the branch was on the water?—
These whom all the years were toward
The golden images the clouds the mountains?

Never before: never in any summer:
Never were days so generous: stars so mild:
Even in old men's talk or in books or remembering
Far back in a gone childhood
Or farther still to the light where Homer wanders—
The air all lucid with the solemn blue
That hills take at the distance beyond change. . . .
That time takes also at the distances.

Never were there promises as now:
Never was green deeper: earth warmer:
Light more beautiful to see: the sound of
Water lovelier: the many forms of
Leaves: stones: clouds: beasts: shadows
Clearer more admirable or the faces
More like answering faces or the hands
Quicker: more brotherly:
                         the aching taste of
Time more salt upon the tongue: more human
Never in any summer: and to whom?

At dusk: by street lights: in the rooms we ask this.

We do not ask for Truth now from John Adams.
We do not ask for Tongues from Thomas Jefferson.
We do not ask for Justice from Tom Paine.
We ask for answers.

And there is an answer.

There is Spain Austria Poland China Bohemia.
There are dead men in the pits in all those countries.
Their mouths are silent but they speak. They say
"The promises are theirs who take them."

Listen! Brothers! Generation!
Listen! You have heard these words. Believe it!
Believe the promises are theirs who take them!

[735]

Believe unless we take them for ourselves
Others will take them for the use of others!

Believe unless we take them for ourselves
All of us: one here: another there:
Men not Man: people not the People:
Hands: mouths: arms: eyes: not syllables—
Believe unless we take them for ourselves
Others will take them: not for us: for others!

Believe unless we take them for ourselves
Now: soon: by the clock: before tomorrow:
Others will take them: not for now: for longer!

Listen! Brothers! Generation!
Companions of leaves: of the sun: of the slow evenings:
Companions of the many days: of all of them:
Listen! Believe the speaking dead! Believe
The journey is our journey. O believe
The signals were to us: the signs: the birds by
Night: the breaking surf.

                 Believe
America is promises to
Take!

America is promises to
Us
To take them
Brutally
With love but
Take them.

O believe this!

MEMORIAL RAIN

by ARCHIBALD MACLEISH

Ambassador Puser the ambassador
Reminds himself in French, felicitous tongue,
What these (young men no longer) lie here for
In rows that once, and somewhere else, were young—

The selections from Archibald MacLeish *Poems 1924-1933* are used by permission of the publishers, Houghton Mifflin Company.

Memorial Rain

All night in Brussels the wind had tugged at my door:
I had heard the wind at my door and the trees strung
Taut, and to me who had never been before
In that country it was a strange wind blowing
Steadily, stiffening the walls, the floor,
The roof of my room. I had not slept for knowing
He too, dead, was a stranger in that land
And felt beneath the earth in the wind's flowing
A tightening of roots and would not understand,
Remembering lake winds in Illinois,
That strange wind. I had felt his bones in the sand
Listening.

        —Reflects that these enjoy
Their country's gratitude, that deep repose,
That peace no pain can break, no hurt destroy,
That rest, that sleep—

                At Ghent the wind rose.
There was a smell of rain and a heavy drag
Of wind in the hedges but not as the wind blows
Over fresh water when the waves lag
Foaming and the willows huddle and it will rain:
I felt him waiting.

        —Indicates the flag
Which (may he say) enisles in Flanders' plain
This little field these happy, happy dead
Have made America—

           In the ripe grain
The wind coiled glistening, darted, fled,
Dragging its heavy body: at Waereghem
The wind coiled in the grass above his head:
Waiting—listening—

        —Dedicates to them
This earth their bones have hallowed, this last gift
A grateful country—

          Under the dry grass stem
The words are blurred, are thickened, the words sift
Confused by the rasp of the wind, by the thin grating

Of ants under the grass, the minute shift
And tumble of dusty sand separating
From dusty sand. The roots of the grass strain,
Tighten, the earth is rigid, waits—he is waiting—

And suddenly, and all at once, the rain!
The living scatter, they run into houses, the wind
Is trampled under the rain, shakes free, is again
Trampled. The rain gathers, running in thinned
Spurts of water that ravel in the dry sand
Seeping in the sand under the grass roots, seeping
Between cracked boards to the bones of a clenched hand:
The earth relaxes, loosens; he is sleeping,
He rests, he is quiet, he sleeps in a strange land.

EPISTLE TO BE LEFT IN THE EARTH

by Archibald MacLeish

. . . It is colder now

               there are many stars

                          we are drifting

North by the Great Bear

                   the leaves are falling

The water is stone in the scooped rocks

                       to southward

Red sun grey air

            the crows are

Slow on their crooked wings

                   the jays have left us

Long since we passed the flares of Orion
Each man believes in his heart he will die
Many have written last thoughts and last letters
None know if our deaths are now or forever
None know if this wandering earth will be found

We lie down and the snow covers our garments
I pray you

            you (if any open this writing)
Make in your mouths the words that were our names

Geography of This Time

I will tell you all we have learned

                         I will tell you everything

The earth is round

              there are springs under the orchards

The loam cuts with a blunt knife

                 beware of

Elms in thunder

           the lights in the sky are stars

We think they do not see

            we think also

The trees do not know nor the leaves of the grasses

                              hear us

The birds too are ignorant

             Do not listen

Do not stand at dark in the open windows

We before you have heard this

                 they are voices

They are not words at all but the wind rising

Also none among us has seen God

(. . . We have thought often

The flaws of sun in the late and driving weather

Pointed to one tree but it was not so)

As for the nights I warn you the nights are dangerous

The wind changes at night and the dreams come

It is very cold

             there are strange stars near Arcturus

Voices are crying an unknown name in the sky

GEOGRAPHY OF THIS TIME

by ARCHIBALD MACLEISH

What is required of us is the recognition of the frontiers between the centuries. And to take heart: to cross over.

Those who are killed in the place between out of ignorance, those who wander like cattle and are shot, those who are shot

From *The New Republic*, Oct. 28, 1942. Reprinted by permission of Mr. Archibald MacLeish and the editors.

and are left in the stone fields between the histories—these men may be pitied as the victims of accidents are pitied but their deaths do not signify. They are neither buried nor otherwise remembered but lie in the dead grass in the dry thorn in the worn light. Their years have no monuments.

There are many such in the sand here— many who did not perceive, who thought the time went on, the years went forward, the history was continuous—who thought tomorrow was of the same nation as today. There are many who came to the frontiers between the times and did not know them —who looked for the sentry-box at the stone bridge, for the barricade in the pines and the declaration in two languages—the warning and the opportunity to turn. They are dead there in the down light, in the sheep's barren.

What is required of us is the recognition

with no sign, with no word, with the

roads raveled out into ruts and the ruts into dust and the dust stirred by the wind —the roads from behind us ending in the dust.

What is required of us is the recognition of the frontiers where the roads end.

We are very far. We are past the place where the light lifts from us and farther on than the relinquishment of leaves—farther even than the persistence in the east of the green color. Beyond are the confused tracks, the guns, the watchers.

What is required of us, Companions, is the recognition of the frontiers across this history, and to take heart: to cross over

—to persist and to cross over and survive

But to survive

To cross over

SPACE BEING CURVED

by E. E. Cummings

Space being(don't forget to remember)Curved
(and that reminds me who said o yes Frost
Something there is which isn't fond of walls)

an electromagnetic (now I've lost
the)Einstein expanded Newton's law preserved
conTinuum(but we read that beFore)

of Course life being just a Reflex you
know since Everything is Relative or

to sum it All Up god being Dead(not to

mention inTerred)
                         LONG LIVE that Upwardlooking
Serene Illustrious and Beatific
Lord of Creation,MAN:
                         at a least crooking
of Whose compassionate digit,earth's most terrific

quadruped swoons into billiardBalls!

O SWEET SPONTANEOUS

by E. E. Cummings

O sweet spontaneous
earth how often have
the
doting
        fingers of
prurient philosophers pinched
and
poked
thee
, has the naughty thumb
of science prodded
thy
        beauty   . how
often have religions taken
thee upon their scraggy knees

squeezing and
buffeting thee that thou mightest
        conceive
gods
        (but
true

to the incomparable
couch of death thy
rhythmic
lover
        thou answerest

them only with

                    spring)

"Well, it looks like a buttercup to me."

NOBODY LOSES ALL THE TIME

by E. E. CUMMINGS

nobody loses all the time

i had an uncle named
Sol who was a born failure and
nearly everybody said he should have gone
into vaudeville perhaps because my Uncle
    Sol could
sing McCann He Was A Diver on Xmas
    Eve like Hell Itself which
may or may not account for the fact that
    my Uncle

Sol indulged in that possibly most inex-
    cusable
of all to use a highfalootin phrase
luxuries that is or to
wit farming and be
it needlessly
added

my Uncle Sol's farm
failed because the chickens
ate the vegetables so
my Uncle Sol had a
chicken farm till the
skunks ate the chickens when

my Uncle Sol
had a skunk farm but
the skunks caught cold and
died so
my Uncle Sol imitated the
skunks in a subtle manner

or by drowning himself in the watertank
but somebody who'd given my Uncle Sol
    a Victor
Victrola and records while he lived pre-
    sented to
him upon the auspicious occasion of his
    decease a
scrumptious not to mention splendiferous
    funeral with
tall boys in black gloves and flowers and
    everything and

i remember we all cried like the Missouri
when my Uncle Sol's coffin lurched be-
    cause
somebody pressed a button
(and down went
my Uncle
Sol

and started a worm farm)

IF YOU CAN'T EAT YOU GOT TO

by E. E. CUMMINGS

If you can't eat you got to

smoke and we aint got
nothing to smoke:come on kid

let's go to sleep
if you can't smoke you got to

Sing and we aint got

nothing to sing;come on kid
let's go to sleep

if you can't sing you got to
die and we aint got

Nothing to die,come on kid

let's go to sleep
if you can't die you got to

dream and we aint got
nothing to dream(come on kid

Let's go to sleep)

SINCE FEELING IS FIRST

by E. E. CUMMINGS

since feeling is first
who pays any attention
to the syntax of things
will never wholly kiss you;

wholly to be a fool
while Spring is in the world

my blood approves,
and kisses are a better fate

than wisdom
lady i swear by all flowers. Don't cry
—the best gesture of my brain is less than
your eyelids' flutter which says

we are for each other: then
laugh, leaning back in my arms
for life's not a paragraph

And death i think is no parenthesis

ANYONE LIVED IN A PRETTY HOW TOWN

by E. E. CUMMINGS

anyone lived in a pretty how town
(with up so floating many bells down)

spring summer autumn winter
he sang his didn't he danced his did.

These Children Singing

Women and men(both little and small)
cared for anyone not at all
they sowed their isn't they reaped their
   same
sun moon stars rain

children guessed(but only a few
and down they forgot as up they grew
autumn winter spring summer)
that noone loved him more by more

when by now and tree by leaf
she laughed his joy she cried his grief
bird by snow and stir by still
anyone's any was all to her

someones married their everyones
laughed their cryings and did their dance
(sleep wake hope and then)they
said their nevers they slept their dream

stars rain sun moon
(and only the snow can begin to explain
how children are apt to forget to re-
   member
with up so floating many bells down)

one day anyone died i guess
(and noone stooped to kiss his face)
busy folk buried them side by side
little by little and was by was

all by all and deep by deep
and more by more they dream their sleep
noone and anyone earth by april
wish by spirit and if by yes.

Women and men(both dong and ding)
summer autumn winter spring
reaped their sowing and went their came
sun moon stars rain

THESE CHILDREN SINGING

by E. E. CUMMINGS

these children singing in stone a
silence of stone these
little children wound with stone
flowers opening for

ever these silently lit
tle children are petals
their song is a flower of
always their flowers

of stone are
silently singing
a song more silent
than silence these always

children forever
singing wreathed with singing
blossoms children of
stone with blossoming

eyes
know if a
lit tle
tree listens

forever to always children singing forever
a song made
of silent as stone silence of
song

LOVE IS MORE THICKER

by E. E. CUMMINGS

love is more thicker than forget
more thinner than recall
more seldom than a wave is wet
more frequent than to fail

it is most mad and moonly
and less it shall unbe
than all the sea which only
is deeper than the sea

love is less always than to win
less never than alive
less bigger than the least begin
less littler than forgive

it is most sane and sunly
and more it cannot die
than all the sky which only
is higher than the sky

WHEN SERPENTS BARGAIN

by E. E. CUMMINGS

when serpents bargain for the right to squirm
and the sun strikes to gain a living wage—
when thorns regard their roses with alarm
and rainbows are insured against old age

when every thrush may sing no new moon in
if all screech-owls have not okayed his voice
—and any wave signs on the dotted line
or else an ocean is compelled to close

when the oak begs permission of the birch
to make an acorn—valleys accuse their
mountains of having altitude—and march
denounces april as a saboteur

then we'll believe in that incredible
unanimal mankind(and not until)

TRAVELOGUE IN A SHOOTING-GALLERY

by KENNETH FEARING

There is a jungle, there is a jungle, there is a vast, vivid, wild, wild, marvelous, marvelous, marvelous jungle,
Open to the public during business hours,
A jungle not very far from an Automat, between a hat store there, and a radio shop.

There, there, whether it rains, or it snows, or it shines,
Under the hot, blazing, cloudless, tropical neon skies that the management always arranges there,
Rows and rows of marching ducks, dozens and dozens and dozens of ducks, move steadily along on smoothly-oiled ballbearing feet,
Ducks as big as telephone books, slow and fearless and out of this world,
While lines and lines of lions, lions, rabbits, panthers, elephants, crocodiles, zebras, apes,
Filled with jungle hunger and jungle rage and jungle love,
Stalk their prey on endless, endless rotary belts through never-ending forests, and burning deserts, and limitless veldts,
To the sound of tom-toms, equipped with silencers, beaten by thousands of savages hidden there.

And there it is that all the big game hunters go, there the traders and the explorers come,
Leanfaced men with windswept eyes who arrive by streetcar, auto or subway, taxi or on foot, streetcar or bus,
And they nod, and they say, and they need no more:
"There . . . there . . .
There they come and there they go."

And weighing machines, in this civilized jungle, will read your soul like an open book, for a penny at a' time, and tell you all,
There, there, where smoking is permitted,
In a jungle that lies, like a rainbow's end, at the very end of every trail,
There, in the only jungle in the whole wide world where ducks are waiting for streetcars,
And hunters can be psychoanalyzed, while they smoke and wait for ducks.

Return to Normal

RECEPTION GOOD

by KENNETH FEARING

Now, at a particular spot on the radio dial, "—in this corner, wearing purple trunks,"
Mingles, somehow, with the news that "—powerful enemy units have been sur-
  rounded in the drive—"
And both of these with the information that "—there is a way to avoid having
  chapped and roughened hands."

Such are the new and complex harmonies, it seems, of a strange and still more
  complex age;
It is not that the reception is confused or poor, but rather it is altogether too clear
  and good,

And no worse, in any case, than that other receiving set, the mind,
Forever faithfully transmitting the great and little impulses that arrive, however
  wavering or loud, from near and far:
"It is an ill wind—" it is apt to report, underscoring this with "—the bigger they
  are the harder they fall," and simultaneously reminding, darkly, that "Things
  are seldom as they seem,"

Reconciling, with ease, the irreconcilable,
Piecing together fragments of a flashing past with clouded snapshots of the present
  and the future,
("Something old, something new," its irrelevant announcer states. "Something bor-
  rowed, something blue.")

Fashioning a raw, wild symphony of a wedding march, a drinking song, and a dirge,
Multiplying enormous figures with precision, then raising the question: But after
  all, what is a man?
Somehow creating hope and fresh courage out of ancient doubt.

"Both boys are on their feet, they're going to it," the radio reports,
"—the sinking was attended by a heavy loss of life—"
"—this amazing cream for quick, miraculous results."

How many pieces are there, in a simple jigsaw puzzle?
How many phases of a man's life can crowd their way into a single moment?
How many angels, actually, can dance on the point of a pin?

NO CREDIT

by KENNETH FEARING

Whether dinner was pleasant, with the windows lit by gunfire, and no one disagreed; or whether, later, we argued in the park, and there was a touch of vomit-gas in the evening air;

Whether we found a greater, deeper, more perfect love, by courtesy of Camels, over NBC; whether the comics amused us, or the newspapers carried a hunger death and a White House prayer for mother's day;

Whether the bills were paid or not, whether or not we had our doubts, whether we spoke our minds at Joe's, and the receipt said "Not Returnable," and the cash-register rang up "No Sale,"

Whether the truth was then, or later, or whether the best had already gone—

Nevertheless, we know; as every turn is measured; as every unavoidable risk is known;

As nevertheless, the flesh grows old, dies, dies in its only life, is gone;

The reflection goes from the mirror; as the shadow, of even a rebel, is gone from the wall;

As nevertheless, the current is thrown and the wheels revolve; and nevertheless, as the word is spoken and the wheat grows tall and the ships sail on—

None but the fool is paid in full; none but the broker, none but the scab is certain of profit;

The sheriff alone may attend a third degree in formal attire; alone, the academy artists multiply in dignity as trooper's bayonet guards the door;

Only Steve, the side-show robot, knows content; only Steve, the mechanical man in love with a photo-electric beam, remains aloof; only Steve, who sits and smokes or stands in salute, is secure;

Steve, whose shoebutton eyes are blind to terror, whose painted ears are deaf to appeal, whose welded breast will never be slashed by bullets, whose armature soul can hold no fear.

PORTRAIT (2)

by KENNETH FEARING

The clear brown eyes, kindly and alert, with 12-20 vision, give confident regard to the passing world through R. K. Lampert & Company lenses framed in gold;
His soul, however, is all his own;

American Rhapsody

Arndt Brothers necktie and hat (with feather) supply a touch of youth.
With his soul his own, he drives, drives, chats and drives,
The first and second bicuspids, lower right, replaced by bridgework, while two in-
cisors have porcelain crowns;

(Render unto Federal, state and city Caesar, but not unto time;
Render nothing unto time until Amalgamated Death serves final notice, in proper
form;

The vault is ready;
The will has been drawn by Clagget, Clagget, Clagget & Brown;
The policies are adequate, Confidential's best, reimbursing for disability, partial or
complete, with double indemnity should the end be a pure and simple accident)

Nothing unto time,
Nothing unto change, nothing unto fate,
Nothing unto you, and nothing unto me, or to any other known or unknown party
or parties, living or deceased;

But Mercury shoes, with special arch supports, take much of the wear and tear;
On the course, a custombuilt driver corrects a tendency to slice;
Love's ravages have been repaired (it was a textbook case) by Drs. Schultz, Light-
ner, Mannheim, and Goode,
While all of it is enclosed in excellent tweed, with Mr. Baumer's personal attention
to the shoulders and the waist;

And all of it now roving, chatting amiably through space in a Plymouth 6.
With his soul (his own) at peace, soothed by Walter Lippmann, and sustained by
Haig & Haig.

AMERICAN RHAPSODY (4)

by KENNETH FEARING

First you bite your fingernails. And then you comb your hair again. And then you
wait. And wait.
(They say, you know, that first you lie. And then you steal, they say. And then,
they say, you kill.)

Then the doorbell rings. Then Peg drops in. And Bill. And Jane. And Doc.
And first you talk, and smoke, and hear the news and have a drink. Then you walk
down the stairs.

And you dine, then, and go to a show after that, perhaps, and after that a night
spot, and after that come home again, and climb the stairs again, and again go
to bed.

But first Peg argues, and Doc replies. First you dance the same dance and you
drink the same drink you always drank before.
And the piano builds a roof of notes above the world.
And the trumpet weaves a dome of music through space. And the drum makes a
ceiling over space and time and night.
And then the table-wit. And then the check. Then home again to bed.
But first, the stairs

And do you now, baby, as you climb the stairs, do you still feel as you felt back
there?
Do you feel again as you felt this morning? And the night before? And then the
night before that?

(They say, you know, that first you hear voices. And then you have visions, they
say. Then, they say, you kick and scream and rave.)
Or do you feel: What is one more night in a lifetime of nights?
What is one more death, or friendship, or divorce out of two, or three? Or four?
Or five?
One more face among so many, many faces, one more life among so many million
lives?

But first, baby, as you climb and count the stairs (and they total the same) did you,
sometime or somewhere, have a different idea?
Is this, baby, what you were born to feel, and do, and be?

READINGS, FORECASTS, PERSONAL GUIDANCE

by KENNETH FEARING

It is not—I swear by every fiery omen to be seen these nights in every quarter of
the heavens, I affirm it by all the monstrous portents of the earth and of the
sea—
It is not that my belief in the true and mystic science is shaken, nor that I have
lost faith in the magic of the cards, or in the augury of dreams, or in the great
and good divinity of the stars.
No, I know still whose science fits the promise to the inquirer's need, invariably, for
a change: Mine. My science foretells the wished-for journey, the business ad-
justment, the handsome stranger. (Each of these is considered a decided change.)

And I know whose skill weighs matrimony, risks a flyer in steel or wheat against the vagaries of the moon.

(Planet of dreams, of mothers and of children, goddess of sailors and of all adventurers, forgive the liberty. But a man must eat.) My skill,

Mine, and the cunning and the patience. (Two dollars for the horoscope in brief and five for a twelve months' forecast in detail.)

No, it is this: The wonders that I have seen with my own eyes.

It is this: That still these people know, as I do not, that what has never been on earth before may still well come to pass,

That always, always there are new and brighter things beneath the sun,

That surely, in bargain basements or in walk-up flats, it must be so that still from time to time they hear wild angel voices speak.

It is this: That I have known them for what they are,

Seen thievery written plainly in their planets, found greed and murder and worse in their birth dates and their numbers, guilt etched in every line of every palm,

But still a light burns through the eyes they turn to me, a need more moving than the damned and dirty dollars (which I must take) that form the pattern of their larger hopes and deeper fears.

And it comes to this: That always I feel another hand, not mine, has drawn and turned the card to find some incredible ace,

Always another word I did not write appears in the spirit parchment prepared by me,

Always another face I do not know shows in the dream, the crystal globe, or the flame.

And finally, this: Corrupt, in a world bankrupt and corrupt, what have I got to do with these miracles?

If they want miracles, let them consult some one else.

Would they, in extremity, ask them of a physician? Or expect them, in desperation, of an attorney? Or of a priest? Or of a poet?

Nevertheless, a man must eat.

Mrs. Raeburn is expected at five. She will communicate with a number of friends and relatives long deceased.

DEVIL'S DREAM

by KENNETH FEARING

But it could never be true;
How could it ever happen, if it never did before, and it's not so now?

But suppose that the face behind those steel prison bars—
Why do you dream about a face lying cold in the trenches streaked with rain and
    dirt and blood?
Is it the very same face seen so often in the mirror?
Just as though it could be true—

But what if it is, what if it is, what if it is, what if the thing that cannot happen
    really happens just the same,
Suppose the fever goes a hundred, then a hundred and one,
What if Holy Savings Trust goes from 98 to 88 to 78 to 68, then drops down to
    28 and 8 and out of sight,
And the fever shoots a hundred two, a hundred three, a hundred four, then a hun-
    dred five and out?

But now there's only the wind and the sky and sunlight and the clouds,
With everyday people walking and talking as they always have before along the
    everyday street,
Doing ordinary things with ordinary faces and ordinary voices in the ordinary way,
Just as they always will—

Then why does it feel like a bomb, why does it feel like a target,
Like standing on the gallows with the trap about to drop,
Why does it feel like a thunderbolt the second before it strikes, why does it feel
    like a tight-rope walk high over hell?

Because it is not, will not, never could be true
That the whole wide, bright, green, warm, calm world goes:
CRASH.

The Express

from Foreword to THE STILL CENTRE
by STEPHEN SPENDER

POETRY does not state truth, it states the conditions within which something felt is true. Even while he is writing about the little portion of reality which is part of his experience, the poet may be conscious of a different reality outside. His problem is to relate the small truth to the sense of a wider, perhaps theoretically known, truth outside his experience. Poems exist within their own limits, they do not exclude the possibility of other things, which might also be subjects of poetry, being different. They remain true to experience and they establish the proportions of that experience. One day a poet will write truthfully about the heroism as well as the fears and anxiety of today; but such a poetry will be very different from the utilitarian heroics of the moment.

I think that there is a certain pressure of external events on poets today, making them tend to write about what is outside their own limited experience. The violence of the times we are living in, the necessity of sweeping and general and immediate action, tend to dwarf the experience of the individual, and to make his immediate environment and occupations perhaps something that he is even ashamed of. For this reason, in my most recent poems, I have deliberately turned back to a kind of writing which is more personal, and I have included within my subjects weakness and fantasy and illusion.

THE EXPRESS
by STEPHEN SPENDER

After the first powerful plain manifesto
The black statement of pistons, without more fuss
But gliding like a queen, she leaves the station.
Without bowing and with restrained unconcern
She passes the houses which humbly crowd outside,
The gasworks and at last the heavy page
Of death, printed by gravestones in the cemetery.
Beyond the town there lies the open country
Where, gathering speed, she acquires mystery,
The luminous self-possession of ships on ocean.
It is now she begins to sing—at first quite low
Then loud, and at last with a jazzy madness—

The song of her whistle screaming at curves,
Of deafening tunnels, brakes, innumerable bolts.
And always light, aerial, underneath
Goes the elate meter of her wheels.
Steaming through metal landscape on her lines
She plunges new eras of wild happiness
Where speed throws up strange shapes, broad curves
And parallels clean like the steel of guns.
At last, further than Edinburgh or Rome,
Beyond the crest of the world, she reaches night
Where only a low streamline brightness
Of phosphorus on the tossing hills is white.
Ah, like a comet through flames she moves entranced
Wrapt in her music no bird song, no, nor bough
Breaking with honey buds, shall ever equal.

NOT PALACES, AN ERA'S CROWN

by STEPHEN SPENDER

Not palaces, an era's crown
Where the mind dwells, intrigues, rests;
The architectural gold-leaved flower
From people ordered like a single mind,
I build. This only what I tell:
It is too late for rare accumulation
For family pride, for beauty's filtered
  dusts;
I say, stamping the words with emphasis,
Drink from here energy and only energy,
As from the electric charge of a battery,
To will this Time's change.
Eye, gazelle, delicate wanderer,
Drinker of horizon's fluid line;
Ear that suspends on a chord
The spirit drinking timelessness;
Touch, love, all senses;
Leave your gardens, your singing feasts,
Your dreams of suns circling before our
  sun,

Of heaven after our world.
Instead, watch images of flashing brass
That strike the outward sense, the pol-
  ished will
Flag of our purpose which the wind en-
  graves.
No spirit seek here rest. But this: No man
Shall hunger: Man shall spend equally.
Our goal which we compel: Man shall be
  man.

—That programme of the antique Satan
Bristling with guns on the indented page
With battleship towering from hilly
  waves:
For what? Drive of a ruining purpose
Destroying all but its age-long exploiters.
Our programme like this, yet opposite,
Death to the killers, bringing light to life.

THE LANDSCAPE NEAR AN AERODROME

by STEPHEN SPENDER

More beautiful and soft than any moth
With burring furred antennae feeling its huge path
Through dusk, the air-liner with shut-off engines
Glides over suburbs and the sleeves set trailing tall
To point the wind. Gently, broadly, she falls
Scarcely disturbing charted currents of air.

Lulled by descent, the travellers across sea
And across feminine land indulging its easy limbs
In miles of softness, now let their eyes trained by watching
Penetrate through dusk the outskirts of this town
Here where industry shows a fraying edge.
Here they may see what is being done.

Beyond the winking masthead light
And the landing-ground, they observe the outposts
Of work: chimneys like lank black fingers
Or figures frightening and mad: and squat buildings
With their strange air behind trees, like women's faces
Shattered by grief. Here where few houses
Moan with faint light behind their blinds
They remark the unhomely sense of complaint, like a dog
Shut out and shivering at the foreign moon.

In the last sweep of love, they pass over fields
Behind the aerodrome, where boys play all day
Hacking dead grass: whose cries, like wild birds,
Settle upon the nearest roofs
But soon are hid under the loud city.

Then, as they land, they hear the tolling bell
Reaching across the landscape of hysteria
To where, larger than all the charcoaled batteries
And imaged towers against that dying sky,
Religion stands, the church blocking the sun.

ULTIMA RATIO REGUM

by STEPHEN SPENDER

The guns spell money's ultimate reason
In letters of lead on the spring hillside.
But the boy lying dead under the olive trees
Was too young and too silly
To have been notable to their important eye.
He was a better target for a kiss.

When he lived, tall factory hooters never summoned him.
Nor did restaurant plate-glass doors revolve to wave him in.
His name never appeared in the papers.
The world maintained its traditional wall
Round the dead with their gold sunk deep as a well,
Whilst his life, intangible as a Stock Exchange rumour, drifted outside.

O too lightly he threw down his cap
One day when the breeze threw petals from the trees.
The unflowering wall sprouted with guns,
Machine-gun anger quickly scythed the grasses;
Flags and leaves fell from hands and branches;
The tweed cap rotted in the nettles.

Consider his life which was valueless
In terms of employment, hotel ledgers, news files.
Consider. One bullet in ten thousand kills a man.
Ask. Was so much expenditure justified
On the death of one so young and so silly
Lying under the olive trees, O world, O death?

from SPIRITUAL EXPLORATIONS

by STEPHEN SPENDER

VI

I am that witness through whom the whole
Knows it exists. Within the coils of blood,
Whispering under sleep, there moves the flood

Of stars, battles, dark and frozen pole.
All that I am I am not. The cold stone
Unfolds its angel for me. On my dreams ride
The racial legends. The stars outside
Glitter under my ribs. Being all, I am alone.
　I who say I call that eye I
Which is the mirror in which things see
Nothing except themselves. I die.
The things, the vision, still will be.
Upon this eye reflections of stars lie
And that which passes, passes away, is I.

I THINK CONTINUALLY OF THOSE WHO WERE TRULY GREAT

by STEPHEN SPENDER

I think continually of those who were truly great.
Who, from the womb, remembered the soul's history
Through corridors of light where the hours are suns
Endless and singing. Whose lovely ambition
Was that their lips, still touched with fire,
Should tell of the Spirit clothed from head to foot in song.
And who hoarded from the Spring branches
The desires falling across their bodies like blossoms.

What is precious is never to forget
The essential delight of the blood drawn from ageless springs
Breaking through rocks in worlds before our earth.
Never to deny its pleasure in the morning simple light
Nor its grave evening demand for love.
Never to allow gradually the traffic to smother
With noise and fog the flowering of the spirit.

Near the snow, near the sun, in the highest fields
See how these names are fêted by the waving grass
And by the streamers of white cloud
And whispers of wind in the listening sky.
The names of those who in their lives fought for life
Who wore at their hearts the fire's centre.
Born of the sun they travelled a short while towards the sun,
And left the vivid air signed with their honour.

from "SQUARES AND OBLONGS" in POETS AT WORK

by W. H. AUDEN

A poet is, before anything else, a person who is passionately in love with language. Whether this love is a sign of his poetic gift or the gift itself—for falling in love is given not chosen—I don't know, but it is certainly the sign by which one recognizes whether a young man is potentially a poet or not.

Two theories of poetry. Poetry as a magical means for inducing desirable emotions and repelling undesirable emotions in oneself and others, or Poetry as a game of knowledge, a bringing to consciousness, by naming them, of emotions and their hidden relationships.

The first view was held by the Greeks, and is now held by MGM, Agit-Prop, and the collective public of the world. They are wrong.

The girl whose boy-friend starts writing her love poems should be on her guard. Perhaps he really does love her, but one thing is certain: while he was writing his poems he was not thinking of her but of his own feeling about her, and that is suspicious. Let her remember St. Augustine's confession of his feelings after the death of someone he loved very much: "I would rather have been deprived of my friend than of my grief."

How can I know what I think till I see what I say? A poet writes "The chestnut's comfortable root" and then changes this to "The chestnut's customary root." In this alteration there is no question of replacing one emotion by another, or of strengthening an emotion, but of discovering what the emotion is. The emotion is unchanged, but waiting to be identified like a telephone number one cannot remember. "8357. No, that's not it. 8557, 8457, no, it's on the tip of my tongue, wait a moment, I've got it, 8657. That's it."

The low-brow says: "I don't like poetry. It requires too much effort to understand and I'm afraid that if I learnt exactly what I feel, it would make me most uncomfortable." He is in the wrong, of course, but not so much in the wrong as the highbrow whose gifts make the effort to understand very little and who, having learned what he feels, is not at all uncomfortable, only interested.

From *Poets at Work,* by W. H. Auden, Karl Shapiro, Rudolf Arnheim, and Donald A. Stauffer, copyright, 1948, by Harcourt, Brace and Company, Inc.

Letter to Lord Byron

NOW THROUGH NIGHT'S CARESSING GRIP
by W. H. AUDEN

Now through night's caressing grip
Earth and all her oceans slip,
Capes of China slide away
From her fingers into day,
And the Americas incline
Coasts toward her shadow line.
Now the ragged vagrants creep
Into crooked holes to sleep;
Just and unjust, worst and best,
Change their places as they rest;
Awkward lovers lie in fields
Where disdainful beauty yields;
While the splendid and the proud
Naked stand before the crowd,
And the losing gambler gains,
And the begger entertains.
May sleep's healing power extend
Through these hours to each friend;
Unpursued by hostile force
Traction engine bull or horse
Or revolting succubus;
Calmly till the morning break
Let them lie, then gently wake.

from LETTER TO LORD BYRON, Part IV
by W. H. AUDEN

The Great War had begun: but masters' scrutiny
　And fists of big boys were the war to us;
It was as harmless as the Indian Mutiny,
　A beating from the Head was dangerous.
　But once when half the form put down *Bellus.*
We were accused of that most deadly sin,
Wanting the Kaiser and the Huns to win.

The way in which we really were affected
　　Was having such a varied lot to teach us.
The best were fighting, as the King expected,
　　The remnant either elderly grey creatures,
　　Or characters with most peculiar features.
Many were raggable, a few were waxy,
One had to leave abruptly in a taxi.

Surnames I must not write—O Reginald,
　　You at least taught us that which fadeth not,
Our earliest visions of the great wide world;
　　The beer and biscuits that your favourites got,
　　Your tales revealing you a first-class shot,
Your riding breeks, your drama called *The Waves,*
A few of us will carry to our graves.

'Half a lunatic, half a knave.' No doubt
　　A holy terror to the staff at tea;
A good headmaster must have soon found out
　　Your moral character was all at sea;
　　I question if you'd got a pass degree:
But little children bless your kind that knocks
Away the edifying stumbling blocks.

How can I thank you? For it only shows
　　(Let me ride just this once my hobby-horse),
There're things a good headmaster never knows.
　　There must be sober schoolmasters, of course,
　　But what a prep school really puts across
Is knowledge of the world we'll soon be lost in:
To-day it's more like Dickens than Jane Austen.

I hate the modern trick, to tell the truth,
　　Of straightening out the kinks in the young mind,
Our passion for the tender plant of youth,
　　Our hatred for all weeds of any kind.
　　Slogans are bad: the best that I can find
Is this: 'Let each child have that's in our care
As much neurosis as the child can bear.'

In this respect, at least, my bad old Adam is
　　Pigheadedly against the general trend;
And has no use for all these new academies
　　Where readers of the better weeklies send
　　The child they probably did not intend,

To paint a lampshade, marry, or keep pigeons,
Or make a study of the world religions.

Goddess of bossy underlings, Normality!
  What murders are committed in thy name!
Totalitarian is thy state Reality,
  Reeking of antiseptics and the shame
  Of faces that all look and feel the same.
Thy Muse is one unknown to classic histories,
The topping figure of the hockey mistress.

From thy dread Empire not a soul's exempted:
  More than the nursemaids pushing prams in parks,
By thee the intellectuals are tempted,
  O, to commit the treason of the clerks,
  Bewitched by thee to literary sharks.
But I must leave thee to thy office stool,
I must get on now to my public school.

Men had stopped throwing stones at one another,
  Butter and Father had come back again;
Gone were the holidays we spent with Mother
  In furnished rooms on mountain, moor, and fen;
  And gone those summer Sunday evenings, when
Along the seafronts fled a curious noise,
'Eternal Father,' sung by three young boys.

Nation spoke Peace, or said she did, with nation;
  The sexes tried their best to look the same;
Morals lost value during the inflation,
  The great Victorians kindly took the blame:
  Visions of Dada to the Post-War came,
Sitting in cafés, nostrils stuffed with bread,
Above the recent and the straight-laced dead.

I've said my say on public schools elsewhere:
  Romantic friendship, prefects, bullying,
I shall not deal with, c'est une autre affaire.
  Those who expect them, will get no such thing,
  It is the strictly relevant I sing.
Why should they grumble? They've the Greek Anthology.
And all the spicier bits of Anthropology.

We all grow up the same way, more or less;
　　Life is not known to give away her presents;
She only swops. The unself-consciousness
　　That children share with animals and peasants
　　Sinks in the 'stürm und drang' of Adolescence.
Like other boys I lost my taste for sweets,
Discovered sunsets, passion, God, and Keats.

I shall recall a single incident
　　No more. I spoke of mining engineering
As the career on which my mind was bent,
　　But for some time my fancies had been veering;
　　Mirages of the future kept appearing;
Crazes had come and gone in short, sharp gales,
For motor-bikes, photography, and whales.

But indecision broke off with a clean-cut end
　　One afternoon in March at half-past three
When walking in a ploughed field with a friend;
　　Kicking a little stone, he turned to me
　　And said, 'Tell me, do you write poetry?'
I never had, and said so, but I knew
That very moment what I wished to do.

Without a bridge passage this leads me straight
　　Into the theme marked 'Oxford' on my score
From pages twenty-five to twenty-eight.
　　Aesthetic trills I'd never heard before
　　Rose from the strings, shrill poses from the cor;
The woodwind chattered like a pre-war Russian,
'Art' boomed the brass, and 'Life' thumped the percussion.

A raw provincial, my good taste was tardy,
　　And Edward Thomas I as yet preferred;
I was still listening to Thomas Hardy
　　Putting divinity about a bird;
　　But Eliot spoke the still unspoken word;
For gasworks and dried tubers I forsook
The clock at Granchester, the English rook.

All youth's intolerant certainty was mine as
　　I faced life in a double-breasted suit;
I bought and praised but did not read Aquinas,

At the *Criterion's* verdict I was mute,
   Though Arnold's I was ready to refute;
And through the quads dogmatic words rang clear,
   'Good poetry is classic and austere.'

So much for Art. Of course Life had its passions too;
   The student's flesh like his imagination
Makes facts fit theories and has fashions too.
   We were the tail, a sort of poor relation
   To that debauched, eccentric generation
That grew up with their fathers at the War,
And made new glosses on the noun Amor.

Three years passed quickly while the Isis went
   Down to the sea for better or for worse;
Then to Berlin, not Carthage, I was sent
   With money from my parents in my purse,
   And ceased to see the world in terms of verse.
I met a chap called Layard and he fed
New doctrines into my receptive head.

Part came from Lane, and part from D. H. Lawrence;
   Gide, though I didn't know it then, gave part.
They taught me to express my deep abhorrence
   If I caught anyone preferring Art
   To Life and Love and being Pure-in-Heart.
I lived with crooks but seldom was molested;
The Pure-in-Heart can never be arrested.

He's gay; no bludgeonings of chance can spoil it,
   The Pure-in-Heart loves all men on a par,
And has no trouble with his private toilet;
   The Pure-in-Heart is never ill; catarrh
   Would be the yellow streak, the brush of tar;
Determined to be loving and forgiving,
I came back home to try and earn my living.

The only thing you never turned your hand to
   Was teaching English in a boarding school.
To-day it's a profession that seems grand to
   Those whose alternative's an office stool;
   For budding authors it's become the rule.
To many an unknown genius postmen bring
Typed notices from Rabbitarse and String.

The Head's M.A., a bishop is a patron,
   The assistant staff is highly qualified;
Health is the care of an experienced matron,
   The arts are taught by ladies from outside;
   The food is wholesome and the grounds are wide;
Their aim is training character and poise,
With special coaching for the backward boys.

I found the pay good and had time to spend it,
   Though others may not have the good luck I did:
For You I'd hesitate to recommend it;
   Several have told me that they can't abide it.
   Still, if one tends to get a bit one-sided,
It's pleasant as it's easy to secure
The hero worship of the immature.

More, it's a job, and jobs to-day are rare:
   All the ideals in the world won't feed us
Although they give our crimes a certain air.
   So barons of the press who know their readers
   Employ to write their more appalling leaders,
Instead of Satan's horned and hideous minions,
Clever young men of liberal opinions.

Which brings me up to nineteen-thirty-five;
   Six months of film work is another story
I can't tell now. But, here I am, alive
   Knowing the true source of that sense of glory
   That still surrounds the England of the Tory,
Come only to the rather tame conclusion
That no man by himself has life's solution.

MUSÉE DES BEAUX ARTS

by W. H. AUDEN

ABOUT suffering they were never wrong,
The Old Masters: how well they understood
Its human position; how it takes place
While someone else is eating or opening a window or just walking dully along;

Law Like Love

How, when the aged are reverently, passionately waiting
For the miraculous birth, there always must be
Children who did not specially want it to happen, skating
On a pond at the edge of the wood:
They never forgot
That even the dreadful martyrdom must run its course
Anyhow in a corner, some untidy spot
Where the dogs go on with their doggy life and the torturer's horse
Scratches its innocent behind on a tree.

In Brueghel's *Icarus,* for instance: how everything turns away
Quite leisurely from the disaster; the ploughman may
Have heard the splash, the forsaken cry,
But for him it was not an important failure; the sun shone
As it had to on the white legs disappearing into the green
Water; and the expensive delicate ship that must have seen
Something amazing, a boy falling out of the sky,
Had somewhere to get to and sailed calmly on.

LAW LIKE LOVE

by W. H. Auden

Law, say the gardeners, is the sun,
Law is the one
All gardeners obey
Tomorrow, yesterday, today.

Law is the wisdom of the old
The impotent grandfathers shrilly scold;
The grandchildren put out a treble tongue,
Law is the senses of the young.

Law, says the priest with a priestly look,
Expounding to an unpriestly people,
Law is the words in my priestly book,
Law is my pulpit and my steeple.

Law, says the judge as he looks down his
nose,
Speaking clearly and most severely,
Law is as I've told you before,
Law is as you know I suppose,
Law is but let me explain it once more,
Law is the Law.

Yet law-abiding scholars write;
Law is neither wrong nor right,
Law is only crimes
Punished by places and by times,
Law is the clothes men wear
Anytime, anywhere,
Law is Good-morning and Good-night.

Others say, Law is our Fate;
Others say, Law is our State;
Others say, others say
Law is no more
Law has gone away.

And always the loud angry crowd
Very angry and very loud
Law is We,
And always the soft idiot softly Me.

If we, dear, know we know no more
Than they about the law,
If I no more than you

[767]

Know what we should and should not do
Except that all agree
Gladly or miserably
That the law is
And that all know this,
If therefore thinking it absurd
To identify Law with some other word.
Unlike so many men
I cannot say Law is again,
No more than they can we suppress
The universal wish to guess
Or slip out of our own position

Into an unconcerned condition.
Although I can at least confine
Your vanity and mine
To stating timidly
A timid similarity
We shall boast anyway:
Like love I say.

Like love we don't know where or why
Like love we can't compel or fly
Like love we often weep
Like love we seldom keep.

CASINO

by W. H. AUDEN

Only the hands are living; to the wheel attracted,
Are moved as deer trek desperately towards a creek
   Through the dust and scrub of the desert, or gently
   As sunflowers turn to the light.

And, as the night takes up the cries of feverish children,
The cravings of lions in dens, the loves of dons,
   Gathers them all and remains the night, the
   Great room is full of their prayers

To the last feast of isolation self-invited
They flock, and in the rite of disbelief are joined;
   From numbers all their stars are recreated,
   The enchanted, the world, the sad.

Without, the rivers flow among the wholly living,
Quite near their trysts; and the mountains part them; and the bird
   Deep in the greens and moistures of summer
   Sings towards their work.

But here no nymph comes naked to the youngest shepherd;
The fountain is deserted; the laurel will not grow;
   The labyrinth is safe but endless, and broken
   Is Ariadne's thread.

As deeper in these hands is grooved their fortune: "Lucky
Were few, and it is possible that none was loved;
   And what was godlike in this generation
   Was never to be born."

PRIME

by W. H. AUDEN

Simultaneously, as soundlessly,
  Spontaneously, suddenly
As, at the vaunt of the dawn, the kind
  Gates of the body fly open
To its world beyond, the gates of the mind,
  The horn gate and the ivory gate
Swing to, swing shut, instantaneously
  Quell the nocturnal rummage
Of its rebellious fronde, ill-favored,
  Ill-natured and second-rate,
Disenfranchised, widowed and orphaned
  By an historical mistake:
Recalled from the shades to be a seeing being,
  From absence to be on display,
Without a name or history I wake
  Between my body and the day.

Holy this moment, wholly in the right,
  As, in complete obedience
To the light's laconic outcry, next
  As a sheet, near as a wall,
Out there as a mountain's poise of stone,
  The world is present, about,
And I know that I am, here, not alone
  But with a world, and rejoice
Unvexed, for the will has still to claim
  This adjacent arm as my own.
The memory to name me, resume
  Its routine of praise and blame,
And smiling to me is this instant while
  Still the day is intact and I
The Adam sinless in our beginning,
  Adam still previous to any act.

I draw breath; that is of course to wish
  No matter what to be wise
To be different to die and the cost
  No matter how is Paradise

Lost of course and myself owing a death:
　The eager ridge, the steady sea,
The flat roofs of the fishing village
　Still asleep in its bunny,
Though as fresh and sunny still are not friends
　But things to hand, this ready flesh
No honest equal but my accomplice now
　My assassin to be and my name
Stands for my historical share of care
　For a lying self-made city,
Afraid of our living task, the dying
　Which the coming day will ask.

NONES

by W. H. Auden

What we know to be not possible,
　Though time after time foretold
By wild hermits, by shaman and sybil
　Gibbering in their trances,
Or revealed to a child in some chance
　rhyme
Like *will* and *kill,* comes to pass
Before we realize it: we are surprised
　At the ease and speed of our deed
And uneasy: It is barely three,
　Mid-afternoon, yet the blood
Of our sacrifice is already
　Dry on the grass; we are not prepared
For silence so sudden and so soon;
　The day is too hot, too bright, too still,
Too ever, the dead remains too nothing.
　What shall we do till nightfall?

The wind has dropped and we have lost
　our public.
　The faceless many who always
Collect when any world is to be wrecked,
　Blown up, burnt down, cracked open,
Felled, sawn in two, hacked through, torn
　apart,
　Have all melted away: not one
Of these who in the shade of walls and
　trees
　Lie sprawled now, calmly sleeping,
Harmless as sheep, can remember why
　He shouted or what about
So loudly in the sunshine this morning;
　All if challenged would reply
—"It was a monster with one red eye,
　A crowd that saw him die, not I."—

The hangman has gone to wash, the sol-
  diers to eat:
 We are left alone with our feat.

The Madonna with the green woodpecker,
  The Madonna of the fig-tree,
The Madonna beside the yellow dam,
  Turn their kind faces from us
And our projects under construction,
  Look only in one direction,
Fix their gaze on our completed work:
  Pile-driver, concrete-mixer,
Crane and pickaxe wait to be used again,
  But how can we repeat this?
Outliving our act, we stand where we are,
  As disregarded as some
Discarded artifact of our own,
  Like torn gloves, rusted kettles,
Abandoned branch-lines, worn lop-sided
  Grindstones buried in nettles.

This mutilated flesh, our victim,
  Explains too nakedly, too well,
The spell of the asparagus-garden,
  The aim of our chalk-pit game; stamps,
Birds' eggs are not the same, behind the
  wonder
Of tow-paths and sunken lanes,
Behind the rapture on the spiral stair,
  We shall always now be aware
Of the deed into which they lead, under
  The mock chase and mock capture,
The racing and tussling and splashing,
  The panting and the laughter,
Be listening for the cry and stillness
  To follow after: wherever
The sun shines, brooks run, books are
  written,
  There will also be this death.

Soon cool tramontana will stir the leaves,
  The shops will re-open at four,
The empty blue bus in the empty pink
  square
  Fill up and depart: we have time

To misrepresent, excuse, deny,
  Mythify, use this event
While, under a hotel bed, in prison,
  Down wrong turnings, its meaning
Waits for our lives: sooner than we would
  choose,
  Bread will melt, water will burn,
And the great quell begin, Abaddon
  Set up his triple gallows
At our seven gates, fat Belial make
  Our wives waltz naked; meanwhile
It would be best to go home, if we have
  a home,
  In any case good to rest.

That our dreaming wills may seem to es-
  cape
  This dead calm, wander instead
On knife edges, on black and white
  squares,
  Across moss, baize, velvet, boards,
Over cracks and hillocks, in mazes
  Of string and penitent cones,
Down granite ramps and damp passages,
  Through gates that will not relatch
And doors marked *Private,* pursued by
  Moors
  And watched by latent robbers,
To hostile villages at the heads of fjords,
  To dark châteaux where wind sobs
In the pine-trees and telephones ring,
  Inviting trouble, to a room,
Lit by one weak bulb, where our Double
  sits
  Writing and does not look up.

That, while we are thus away, our own
  wronged flesh
  May work undisturbed, restoring
The order we try to destroy, the rhythm
  We spoil out of spite: valves close
And open exactly, glands secrete,
  Vessels contract and expand
At the right moment, essential fluids
  Flow to renew exhausted cells,

Not knowing quite what has happened,
  but awed
By death like all the creatures
Now watching this spot, like the hawk
  looking down

Without blinking, the smug hens
Passing close by in their pecking order,
  The bug whose view is balked by grass,
Or the deer who shyly from afar
  Peer through chinks in the forest.

UNDER WHICH LYRE

A Reactionary Tract for the Times
(Phi Beta Kappa Poem. Harvard. 1946)

by W. H. AUDEN

Ares at last has quit the field,
The bloodstains on the bushes yield
    To seeping showers,
And in their convalescent state
The fractured towns associate
    With summer flowers.

Encamped upon the college plain
Raw veterans already train
    As freshman forces;
Instructors with sarcastic tongue
Shepherd the battle-weary young
    Through basic courses.

Among bewildering appliances
For mastering the arts and sciences
    They stroll or run,
And nerves that never flinched at slaughter
Are shot to pieces by the shorter
    Poems of Donne.

Under Which Lyre

Professors back from secret missions
Resume their proper eruditions,
    Though some regret it;
They liked their dictaphones a lot,
They met some big wheels, and do not
    Let you forget it.

But Zeus' inscrutable decree
Permits the will-to-disagree
    To be pandemic,
Ordains that vaudeville shall preach
And every commencement speech
    Be a polemic.

Let Ares doze, that other war
Is instantly declared once more
    'Twixt those who follow
Precocious Hermes all the way
And those who without qualms obey
    Pompous Apollo.

Brutal like all Olympic games,
Though fought with smiles and Christian names
    And less dramatic,
This dialectic strife between
The civil gods is just as mean,
    And more fanatic.

What high immortals do in mirth
Is life and death on Middle Earth;
    Their a-historic
Antipathy forever gripes
All ages and somatic types,
    The sophomoric

Who face the future's darkest hints
With giggles or with prairie squints
    As stout as Cortez,
And those who like myself turn pale
As we approach with ragged sail
    The fattening forties.

The sons of Hermes love to play,
And only do their best when they
    Are told they oughtn't;

Apollo's children never shrink
From boring jobs but have to think
    Their work important.

Related by antithesis,
A compromise between us is
    Impossible;
Respect perhaps but friendship never:
Falstaff the fool confronts forever
    The prig Prince Hal.

If he would leave the self alone,
Apollo's welcome to the throne,
    Fasces and falcons;
He loves to rule, has always done it;
The earth would soon, did Hermes run it,
    Be like the Balkans.

But jealous of our god of dreams,
His common-sense in secret schemes
    To rule the heart;
Unable to invent the lyre,
Creates with simulated fire
    Official art.

And when he occupies a college,
Truth is replaced by Useful Knowledge;
    He pays particular
Attention to Commercial Thought,
Public Relations, Hygiene, Sport,
    In his curricula

Athletic, extrovert and crude,
For him, to work in solitude
    Is the offence,
The goal a populous Nirvana:
His shield bears this device: *Mens sana*
    Qui mal y pense.

Today his arms, we must confess,
From Right to Left have met success,
    His banners wave
From Yale to Princeton, and the news
From Broadway to the Book Reviews
    Is very grave.

Under Which Lyre

His radio Homers all day long
In over-Whitmanated song
        That does not scan,
With adjectives laid end to end,
Extol the doughnut and commend
        The Common Man.

His, too, each homely lyric thing
On sport or spousal love or spring
        Or dogs or dusters,
Invented by some court-house bard
For recitation by the yard
        In filibusters.

To him ascend the prize orations
And sets of fugal variations
        On some folk-ballad,
While dietitians sacrifice
A glass of prune-juice or a nice
        Marsh-mallow salad.

Charged with his compound of sensational
Sex plus some undenominational
        Religious matter,
Enormous novels by co-eds
Rain down on our defenceless heads
        Till our teeth chatter.

In fake Hermetic uniforms
Behind our battle-line, in swarms
        That keep alighting,
His existentialists declare
That they are in complete despair,
        Yet go on writing.

No matter; He shall be defied;
White Aphrodite is on our side:
        What though his threat
To organize us grow more critical?
Zeus willing, we, the unpolitical,
        Shall beat him yet.

Lone scholars, sniping from the walls
Of learned periodicals,
        Our facts defend,

Our intellectual marines,
Landing in little magazines
    Capture a trend.

By night our student Underground
At cocktail parties whisper round
    From ear to ear;
Fat figures in the public eye
Collapse next morning, ambushed by
    Some witty sneer.

In our morale must lie our strength:
So, that we may behold at length
    Routed Apollo's
Battalions melt away like fog,
Keep well the Hermetic Decalogue,
    Which runs as follows:—

Thou shalt not do as the dean pleases,
Thou shalt not write thy doctor's thesis
    On education,
Thou shalt not worship projects nor
Shalt thou or thine bow down before
    Administration.

Thou shalt not answer questionnaires
Or quizzes upon World-Affairs,
    Nor with compliance
Take any test. Thou shalt not sit
With statisticians nor commit
    A social science.

Thou shalt not be on friendly terms
With guys in advertising firms,
    Nor speak with such
As read the Bible for its prose,
Nor, above all, make love to those
    Who wash too much.

Thou shalt not live within thy means
Nor on plain water and raw greens.
    If thou must choose
Between the chances, choose the odd;
Read *The New Yorker,* trust in God;
    And take short views.

from SELECTED WRITINGS
by DYLAN THOMAS

Poetry is the rhythmic, inevitably narrative, movement from an over-clothed blindness to a naked vision . . . the physical and mental task of constructing a formally watertight compartment of words. . . . Poetry must drag further into the clear nakedness of light more even of the hidden causes than Freud could realize.

IN MY CRAFT OR SULLEN ART
by DYLAN THOMAS

In my craft or sullen art
Exercised in the still night
When only the moon rages
And the lovers lie abed
With all their griefs in their arms,
I labour by singing light
Not for ambition or bread
Or the strut and trade of charms
On the ivory stages
But for the common wages

Of their most secret heart.
Not for the proud man apart
From the raging moon I write
On these spindrift pages
Not for the towering dead
With their nightingales and psalms
But for the lovers, their arms
Round the griefs of the ages,
Who pay no praise or wages
Nor heed my craft or art.

"THE HAND THAT SIGNED THE PAPER FELLED A CITY"
by DYLAN THOMAS

The hand that signed the paper felled a city;
Five sovereign fingers taxed the breath,
Doubled the globe of dead and halved a country;
These five kings did a king to death.

The mighty hand leads to a sloping shoulder,
The finger joints are cramped with chalk;
A goose's quill has put an end to murder
That put an end to talk.

The hand that signed the treaty bred a fever,
And famine grew, and locusts came;
Great is the hand that holds dominion over
Man by a scribbled name.

The five kings count the dead but do not soften
The crusted wound nor pat the brow;
A hand rules pity as a hand rules heaven;
Hands have no tears to flow.

POEM IN OCTOBER

by DYLAN THOMAS

It was my thirtieth year to heaven
Woke to my hearing from harbour and neighbour wood
   And the mussel pooled and the heron
      Priested shore
     The morning beckon
With water praying and call of seagull and rook
And the knock of sailing boats on the net webbed wall
    Myself to set foot
      That second
In the still sleeping town and set forth.

My birthday began with the water-
Birds and the birds of the winged trees flying my name
   Above the farms and the white horses
      And I rose
     In rainy autumn
And walked abroad in a shower of all my days.
High tide and the heron dived when I took the road
    Over the border
      And the gates
Of the town closed as the town awoke.

A springful of larks in a rolling
Cloud and the roadside bushes brimming with whistling
   Blackbirds and the sun of October
      Summery
     On the hill's shoulder,
Here were fond climates and sweet singers suddenly
Come in the morning where I wandered and listened
    To the rain wringing
      Wind blow cold
In the wood faraway under me.

Pale rain over the dwindling harbour
And over the sea wet church the size of a snail
   With its horns through mist, and the castle
      Brown as owls,
     But all the gardens
Of spring and summer were blooming in the tall tales

Poem in October

Beyond the border and under the lark full cloud.
   There could I marvel
     My birthday
Away but the weather turned around.

  It turned away from the blithe country
And down the other air and the blue altered sky
  Streamed again a wonder of summer
     With apples
   Pears and red currants
And I saw in the turning so clearly a child's
Forgotten mornings when he walked with his mother
    Through the parables
     Of sun light
   And the legends of the green chapels

  And the twice told fields of infancy
That his tears burned my cheeks and his heart moved in mine.
  These were the woods the river and sea
     Where a boy
    In the listening
Summertime of the dead whispered the truth of his joy
To the trees and the stones and the fish in the tide.
    And the mystery
     Sang alive
Still in the water and singing birds.

  And there could I marvel my birthday
Away but the weather turned around. And the true
  Joy of the long dead child sang burning
     In the sun.
   It was my thirtieth
Year to heaven stood there then in the summer noon
Though the town below lay leaved with October blood.
    O may my heart's truth
     Still be sung
  On this high hill in a year's turning.

IN THE WHITE GIANT'S THIGH
by Dylan Thomas

Through throats where many rivers meet, the curlews cry,
Under the conceiving moon, on the high chalk hill,
And there this night I walk in the white giant's thigh
Where barren as boulders women lie longing still

To labour and love though they lay down long ago.

Through throats where many rivers meet, the women pray,
Pleading in the waded bay for the seed to flow
Though the names on their weed grown stones are rained away,

And alone in the night's eternal, curving act
They yearn with tongues of curlews for the unconceived
And immemorial sons of the cudgelling, hacked

Hill. Who once in gooseskin winter loved all ice leaved
In the courters' lanes, or twined in the ox roasting sun
In the wains tonned so high that the wisps of the hay
Clung to the pitching clouds, or gay with any one
Young as they in the after milking moonlight lay

Under the lighted shapes of faith and their moonshade
Petticoats galed high, or shy with the rough riding boys,
Now clasp me to their grains in the gigantic glade,

Who once, green countries since, were a hedgerow of joys.
Time by, their dust was flesh the swineherd rooted sly,
Flared in the reek of the wiving sty with the rush
Light of his thighs, spreadeagle to the dunghill sky,
Or with their orchard man in the core of the sun's bush
Rough as cows' tongues and thrashed with brambles their buttermilk
Manes, under his quenchless summer barbed gold to the bone,

Or rippling soft in the spinney moon as the silk
And ducked and draked white lake that harps to a hail stone.

Who once were a bloom of wayside brides in the hawed house
And heard the lewd, wooed field flow to the coming frost,

In the White Giant's Thigh

The scurrying, furred small friars squeal, in the dowse
Of day, in the thistle aisles, till the white owl crossed

Their breast, the vaulting does roister, the horned bucks climb
Quick in the wood at love, where a torch of foxes foams,
All birds and beasts of the linked night uproar and chime

And the mole snout blunt under his pilgrimage of domes,
Or, butter fat goosegirls, bounced in a gambo bed,
Their breasts full of honey, under their gander king
Trounced by his wings in the hissing shippen, long dead
And gone that barley dark where their clogs danced in the spring,
And their firefly hairpins flew, and the ricks ran round—

(But nothing bore, no mouthing babe to the veined hives
Hugged, and barren and bare on Mother Goose's ground
They with the simple Jacks were a boulder of wives)—

Now curlew cry me down to kiss the mouths of their dust.

The dust of their kettles and clocks swings to and fro
Where the hay rides now or the bracken kitchens rust
As the arc of the billhooks that flashed the hedges low
And cut the birds' boughs that the minstrel sap ran red.
They from houses where the harvest kneels, hold me hard,
Who heard the tall bell sail down the Sundays of the dead
And the rain wring out its tongues on the faded yard,
Teach me the love that is evergreen after the fall leaved
Grave, after Belovèd on the grass gulfed cross is scrubbed
Off by the sun and Daughters no longer grieved
Save by their long desirers in the fox cubbed
Streets or hungering in the crumbled wood: to these
Hale dead and deathless do the women of the hill
Love for ever meridian through the courters' trees

And the daughters of darkness flame like Fawkes fires still.

ON NO WORK OF WORDS
by DYLAN THOMAS

On no work of words now for three lean months in the bloody
Belly of the rich year and the big purse of my body
I bitterly take to task my poverty and craft:

To take to give is all, return what is hungrily given
Puffing the pounds of manna up through the dew to heaven,
The lovely gift of the gab bangs back on a blind shaft.

To lift to leave from the treasures of man is pleasing death
That will rake at last all currencies of the marked breath
And count the taken, forsaken mysteries in a bad dark.

To surrender now is to pay the expensive ogre twice.
Ancient woods of my blood, dash down to the nut of the seas
If I take to burn or return this world which is each man's work.

POEM ON HIS BIRTHDAY
by DYLAN THOMAS

In the mustardseed sun,
By full tilt river and switchback sea
  Where the cormorants scud,
In his house on stilts high among beaks
  And palavers of birds
This sandgrain day in the bent bay's grave
  He celebrates and spurns
His driftwood thirty-fifth wind turned
  age;
  Herons spire and spear.

Under and round him go
Flounders, gulls, on their cold, dying
  trails,
  Doing what they are told,

Curlews aloud in the congered waves
  Work at their ways to death,
And the rhymer in the long tongued
  room,
  Who tolls his birthday bell,
Toils towards the ambush of his wounds;
  Herons, steeple stemmed, bless.

In the thistledown fall,
He sings towards anguish; finches fly
  In the claw tracks of hawks
On a seizing sky; small fishes glide
  Through wynds and shells of drowned
Ship towns to pastures of otters. He
  In his slant, racking house

And the hewn coils of his trade perceives
  Herons walk in their shroud,

  The livelong river's robe
Of minnows wreathing around their
    prayer;
  And far at sea he knows,
Who slaves to his crouched, eternal end
  Under a serpent cloud,
Dolphins dive in their turnturtle dust,
  The rippled seals streak down
To kill and their own tide daubing blood
  Slides good in the sleek mouth.

  In a cavernous, swung
Wave's silence, wept white angelus knells.
  Thirty-five bells sing struck
On skull and scar where his loves lie
    wrecked,
  Steered by the falling stars.
And to-morrow weeps in a blind cage
  Terror will rage apart
Before chains break to a hammer flame
  And love unbolts the dark

  And freely he goes lost
In the unknown, famous light of great
  And fabulous, dear God.
Dark is a way and light is a place,
  Heaven that never was
Nor will be ever is always true,
  And, in that brambled void,
Plenty as blackberries in the woods
  The dead grow for His joy.

  There he might wander bare
With the spirits of the horseshoe bay
  Or the stars' seashore dead,
Marrow of eagles, the roots of whales
  And wishbones of wild geese,
With blessed, unborn God and His Ghost,
  And every soul His priest,

Gulled and chanter in young Heaven's
    fold
  Be at cloud quaking peace,

  But dark is a long way.
He, on the earth of the night, alone
  With all the living, prays,
Who knows the rocketing wind will blow
  The bones out of the hills,
And the scythed boulders bleed, and the
    last
  Rage shattered waters kick
Masts and fishes to the still quick stars,
  Faithlessly unto Him

  Who is the light of old
And air shaped Heaven where souls grow
    wild
  As horses in the foam:
Oh, let me midlife mourn by the shrined
  And druid herons' vows
The voyage to ruin I must run,
  Dawn ships clouted aground,
Yet, though I cry with tumbledown
    tongue,
  Count my blessings aloud:

  Four elements and five
Senses, and man a spirit in love
  Tangling through this spun slime
To his nimbus bell cool kingdom come
  And the lost, moonshine domes,
And the sea that hides his secret selves
  Deep in its black, base bones,
Lulling of spheres in the seashell flesh,
  And this last blessing most,

  That the closer I move
To death, one man through his sundered
    hulks,
  The louder the sun blooms
And the tusked, ramshackling sea exults;
  And every wave of the way
And gale I tackle, the whole world then,
  With more triumphant faith

[783]

Than ever was since the world was said,
  Spins its morning of praise,

I hear the bouncing hills
Grow larked and greener at berry brown
  Fall and the dew larks sing

Taller this thunderclap spring, and how
  More spanned with angels ride
The mansouled fiery islands! Oh,
  Holier then their eyes,
And my shining men no more alone
  As I sail out to die.

A WINTER'S TALE
by DYLAN THOMAS

  It is a winter's tale
That the snow blind twilight ferries over the lakes
And floating fields from the farm in the cup of the vales,
Gliding windless through the hand folded flakes,
The pale breath of cattle at the stealthy sail,

  And the stars falling cold,
And the smell of hay in the snow, and the far owl
Warning among the folds, and the frozen hold
Flocked with the sheep white smoke of the farm house cowl
In the river wended vales where the tale was told.

  Once when the world turned old
On a star of faith pure as the drifting bread,
As the food and flames of the snow, a man unrolled
The scrolls of fire that burned in his heart and head,
Torn and alone in a farm house in a fold

  Of fields. And burning then
In his firelit island ringed by the winged snow
And the dung hills white as wool and the hen
Roosts sleeping chill till the flame of the cock crow
Combs through the mantled yards and the morning men

  Stumble out with their spades,
The cattle stirring, the mousing cat stepping shy,
The puffed birds hopping and hunting, the milk maids
Gentle in their clogs over the fallen sky,
And all the woken farm at its white trades,

A Winter's Tale

He knelt, he wept, he prayed,
By the spit and the black pot in the log bright light
And the cup and the cut bread in the dancing shade,
In the muffled house, in the quick of night,
At the point of love, forsaken and afraid.

He knelt on the cold stones,
He wept from the crest of grief, he prayed to the veiled sky
May his hunger go howling on bare white bones
Past the statues of the stables and the sky roofed sties
And the duck pond glass and the blinding byres alone

Into the home of prayers
And fires where he should prowl down the cloud
Of his snow blind love and rush in the white lairs.
His naked need struck him howling and bowed
Though no sound flowed down the hand folded air

But only the wind strung
Hunger of birds in the fields of the bread of water, tossed
In high corn and the harvest melting on their tongues.
And his nameless need bound him burning and lost
When cold as snow he should run the wended vales among

The rivers mouthed in night,
And drown in the drifts of his need, and lie curled caught
In the always desiring center of the white
Inhuman cradle and the bride bed forever sought
By the believer lost and the hurled outcast of light.

Deliver him, he cried,
By losing him all in love, and cast his need
Alone and naked in the engulfing bride,
Never to flourish in the fields of the white seed
Or flower under the time dying flesh astride.

Listen. The minstrels sing
In the departed villages. The nightingale,
Dust in the buried wood, flies on the grains of her wings
And spells on the winds of the dead his winter's tale.
The voice of the dust of water from the withered spring

Is telling. The wizened
Stream with bells and baying water bounds. The dew rings

On the gristed leaves and the long gone glistening
Parish of snow. The carved mouths in the rock are wind swept strings.
Time sings through the intricately dead snow drop. Listen.

It was a hand or sound
In the long ago land that glided the dark door wide
And there outside on the bread of the ground
A she bird rose and rayed like a burning bride.
A she bird dawned, and her breast with snow and scarlet downed.

Look. And the dancers move
On the departed, snow bushed green, wanton in moon light
As a dust of pigeons. Exulting, the grave hooved
Horses, centaur dead, turn and tread the drenched white
Paddocks in the farms of birds. The dead oak walks for love.

The carved limbs in the rock
Leap, as to trumpets. Calligraphy of the old
Leaves is dancing. Lines of age on the stones weave in a flock.
And the harp shaped voice of the water's dust plucks in a fold
Of fields. For love, the long ago she bird rises. Look.

And the wild wings were raised
Above her folded head, and the soft feathered voice
Was flying through the house as though the she bird praised
And all the elements of the slow fall rejoiced
That a man knelt alone in the cup of the vales,

In the mantle and calm,
By the spit and the black pot in the log bright light.
And the sky of birds in the plumed voice charmed
Him up and he ran like a wind after the kindling flight
Past the blind barns and byres of the windless farm.

In the poles of the year
When black birds died like priests in the cloaked hedge row
And over the cloth of counties the far hills rode near,
Under the one leaved trees ran a scarecrow of snow
And fast through the drifts of the thickets antlered like deer,

Rags and prayers down the knee-
Deep hillocks and loud on the numbed lakes,
All night lost and long wading in the wake of the she-
Bird through the times and lands and tribes of the slow flakes.
Listen and look where she sails the goose plucked sea,

A Winter's Tale

The sky, the bird, the bride,
The cloud, the need, the planted stars, the joy beyond
The fields of seed and the time dying flesh astride,
The heavens, the heaven, the grave, the burning font.
In the far ago land the door of his death glided wide,

And the bird descended.
On a bread white hill over the cupped farm
And the lakes and floating fields and the river wended
Vales where he prayed to come to the last harm
And the home of prayers and fires, the tale ended.

The dancing perishes
On the white, no longer growing green, and, minstrel dead,
The singing breaks in the snow shoed villages of wishes
That once cut the figures of birds on the deep bread
And over the glazed lakes skated the shapes of fishes

Flying. The rite is shorn
Of nightingale and centaur dead horse. The springs wither
Back. Lines of age sleep on the stones till trumpeting dawn.
Exultation lies down. Time buries the spring weather
That belled and bounded with the fossil and the dew reborn.

For the bird lay bedded
In a choir of wings, as though she slept or died,
And the wings glided wide and he was hymned and wedded,
And through the thighs of the engulfing bride,
The woman breasted and the heaven headed

Bird, he was brought low
Burning in the bride bed of love, in the whirl-
Pool at the wanting center, in the folds
Of paradise, in the spun bud of the world.
And she rose with him flowering in her melting snow.

DO NOT GO GENTLE INTO THAT GOOD NIGHT

by DYLAN THOMAS

Do not go gentle into that good night,
Old age should burn and rave at close of day;
Rage, rage against the dying of the light.

Though wise men at their end know dark is right,
Because their words had forked no lightning they
Do not go gentle into that good night.

Good men, the last wave by, crying how bright
Their frail deeds might have danced in a green bay,
Rage, rage against the dying of the light.

Wild men who caught and sang the sun in flight,
And learn, too late, they grieved it on its way,
Do not go gentle into that good night.

Grave men, near death, who see with blinding sight
Blind eyes could blaze like meteors and be gay,
Rage, rage against the dying of the light.

And you, my father, there on the sad height,
Curse, bless, me now with your fierce tears, I pray.
Do not go gentle into that good night.
Rage, rage against the dying of the light.

A Girl in the Snow (For T.)

GUIDED MISSILES EXPERIMENTAL RANGE

by ROBERT CONQUEST

Soft sounds and odours brim up through the night
A wealth below the level of the eye;
Out of a black, an almost violet sky
Abundance flowers into points of light.

Till from the south-west, as their low scream mars
And halts this warm hypnosis of the dark,
Three black automata cut swift and stark,
Shaped clearly by the backward flow of stars.

Stronger than lives, by empty purpose blinded,
The only thought their circuits can endure is
The target-hunting rigour of their flight;

And by that loveless haste I am reminded
Of Aeschylus' description of the Furies:
"O barren daughters of the fruitful night."

A GIRL IN THE SNOW (For T.)

by ROBERT CONQUEST

Autumn's attrition. Then this world laid waste
Under a low white sky, diffusing glare
On blurs of snow as motionless and bare
As the dead epoch where our luck is placed.

Till from the imprecise close distance flies,
Winged on your skis and stillness-breaking nerve
Colour, towards me down this vital curve,
Blue suit, bronze hair and honey-coloured eyes.

Under this hollow cloud, a sky of rime,
The eyes' one focus in an empty mirror
You come towards my arms until I hold

Close to my heart, beyond all fear and error,
A clear-cut warmth in this vague waste of cold:
A road of meaning through the shapeless time.

From *Poems*, by Robert Conquest; reprinted by permission of Macmillan & Company Ltd., and St. Martin's Press.

A LEVEL OF ABSTRACTION

by ROBERT CONQUEST

Summer, stream and stillness:
A solstice of the heart
Where she calls to its fullness
That endless search, that art.

The clear sweet known stream
Could not abstract to absolute
Crystal: he broke from that dream
A heart made desolate
In preparation for
Extremes of fruitfulness.

Briefly a kingfisher
Slashes the motionless
Vision of soft grey water
Where grey-green willows bend
With violent speed and colour.

And yet is congruent
To blue deep clarities
Of a delighting mind
As he looks deep into eyes
Through which strong virtues bind
Into the body's grace
The reciprocal beauties
Of her heart and face.

The apparatus of paradise
Is here, is made their own.
Roses and dragonflies
Glow on water or lawn;
The gold leaf does not move;
The soft air has not stirred;
She stands, the form of love.

Love is a general word.

EPISTEMOLOGY OF POETRY

by ROBERT CONQUEST

Across the long-curved bight or bay
The waves move clear beneath the day
And, rolling in obliquely, each
Unwinds its white torque up the beach.

Beneath the full semantic sun
The twisting currents race and run.
Words and evaluations start,
And yet the verse should play its part.

Below a certain threshold light
Is insufficient to excite
Those mechanisms which the eye
Constructs its daytime objects by:

A different system wakes behind
The dark, wide pupils till the mind
Accepts an image of this sea
As clear, but in an altered key.

Now darkness falls. And poems attempt
Light reconciling done and dreamt.
I do not find it in the rash
Disruption of the lightning flash.

Those vivid rigours stun the verse
And neural structure still prefers
The moon beneath whose moderate light
The great seas glitter in the bight.

HUMANITIES

by Robert Conquest

Hypnotized and told they're seeing red
When really looking at a yellow wall
The children speak of orange seen instead:
Split to such rainbow through that verbal lens
It takes a whole heart's effort to see all
The human plenum as a single ens.

The word on the objective breath must be
A wind to winnow the emotive out;
Music can generalize the inner sea
In dark harmonics of the blinded heart;
But, hot with certainty and keen with doubt,
Verse sweats out heartfelt knowledge, clear-eyed art.

Is it, when paper roses make us sneeze,
A mental or a physical event?
The word can freeze us to such categories,
Yet verse can warm the mirrors of the word
And through their loose distortions represent
The scene, the heart, the life, as they occurred.

—In a dream's blueness or a sunset's bronze
Poets seek the images of love and wonder,
But absolutes of music, gold or swans
Are only froth unless they go to swell
That harmony of science pealing under
The poem's waters like a sunken bell.

CHILD WAKING

by E. J. Scovell

The child sleeps in the daytime,
With his abandoned, with his jetsam look,
On the bare mattress, across the cot's corner;
Covers and toys thrown out, a routine labour.

Relaxed in sleep and light,
Face upwards, never so clear a prey to eyes;
Like a walled town surprised out of the air
All life called in, yet all laid bare

To the enemy above—
He has taken cover in daylight, gone to ground
In his own short length, his body strong in bleached
Blue cotton and his arms outstretched.

From *The River Steamer*, 1956. Reprinted by permission of The Cresset Press.

Now he opens eyes but not
To see at first; they reflect the light like snow,
And I wait in doubt if he sleeps or wakes, till I see
Slight pain of effort at the boundary,

And hear how the trifling wound
Of bewilderment fetches a caverned cry
As he crosses out of sleep—at once to recover
His place and poise, and smile as I lift him over.

But I recall the blue-
White snowfield of his eyes empty of sight
High between dream and day, and think how there
The soul might rise visible as a flower.

The Piper   Eugene Harris
Courtesy of *POPULAR PHOTOGRAPHY*

GENESIS

by Geoffrey Hill

I

Against the burly air I strode,
Where the tight ocean heaves its load,
Crying the miracles of God.

And first I brought the sea to bear
Upon the dead weight of the land;
And the waves flourished at my prayer,
The rivers spawned their sand.

And where the streams were salt and full
The tough pig-headed salmon strove,
Curbing the ebb and the tide's pull,
To reach the steady hills above.

II

The second day I stood and saw
The osprey plunge with triggered claw,
Feathering blood along the shore,
To lay the living sinew bare.

And the third day I cried: "Beware
The soft-voiced owl, the ferret's smile,
The hawk's deliberate stoop in air,
Cold eyes, and bodies hooped in steel,
Forever bent upon the kill."

III

And I renounced, on the fourth day,
This fierce and unregenerate clay,

Building as a huge myth for man
The watery Leviathan,

And made the glove-winged albatross
Scour the ashes of the sea
Where Capricorn and Zero cross,
A brooding immortality—
Such as the charmed phoenix has
In the unwithering tree.

IV

The phoenix burns as cold as frost;
And, like a legendary ghost,
The phantom-bird goes wild and lost,
Upon a pointless ocean tossed.

So, the fifth day, I turned again
To flesh and blood and the blood's pain.

V

On the sixth day, as I rode
In haste about the works of God,
With spurs I plucked the horse's blood.

By blood we live, the hot, the cold,
To ravage and redeem the world:
There is no bloodless myth will hold.

And by Christ's blood are men made free
Though in close shrouds their bodies lie
Under the rough pelt of the sea;

Though Earth has rolled beneath her
  weight
The bones that cannot bear the light.

Reprinted by permission of Geoffrey Hill and Andre Deutsch Ltd.

TIME AND MOTION STUDY

by IAIN FLETCHER

What are they? Why, only qualities of
    light
That once or twice were fractured into
    form:
Short wisps or rags that sting the touch
    or sight,
Dancing in famine through a night of
    storm:
    Cold images of Heat corrupt within,
    Whose mercies rattle in a bowl of tin.

But being not worshipped, being forgot-
    ten, brood
In eyes that fire the night with mysteries
And drag the heart to manufacture good
Where no good thing was ever held to
    rise:
    What I would do, I do not, doing
    All that I hate; pursued, myself pursu-
      ing.

Hunting myself in others, hunting what
Was never life to be quarry, only sired—
Member of darkness—by a swirling phan-
    tom, not
That warmth and tenseness have desired,
    Gifts never nourished by my cruel arts:
    A blinding Grace can only crack dry
    hearts.

But these all breathe out "illusion," are
Heavily unreal, a drugged metaphysician,
Plotting a marriage of retina and star
At some rare locus that is not position.
    Somewhere to find that sweet duality
    Of mind and flesh the heart would mag-
      nify.

My life is after Fall and Flood and Pas-
    sion,
When Prophets wither into irony;
When the dead cosmos in a formal fash-
    ion
Translates all grievings into vanity,
    My life is after Unity, and wanders still
    In penitential valleys of the will.

A cradle swayed under a barren roof,
Or on the waves where Orpheus sowed
    his faith;
The horned God raging on a bull's black
    hoof.
My life lies in the diocese of wraith,
    My life lies after wrath, being so unreal
    There are no darker flashes to conceal.

Nor the severities of beauty, nor
The haunting disk of one occulted face;
The moral charm that all too many wore,
Too pertinently confident of Grace,
    My life is after Space and Time and
    Will,
    My life is always moved, but always
    still,

None moves me but my weakness, weak
Beyond all judgment, as beyond all law;
How should I ask for witnesses to speak,
Tethered in graves, watchmen who never
    saw,
    But in their majesty of distance gave
    Me mandate to believe these sighs might
    save.

Reprinted by permission of Iain Fletcher.

MASTERS

by KINGSLEY AMIS

That horse whose rider fears to jump will fall,
Riflemen miss if orders sound unsure;
They only are secure who seem secure;
   Who lose their voice, lose all.

Those whom heredity or guns have made
Masters, must show it by a common speech;
Expected words in the same tone from each
   Will always be obeyed.

Likewise with stance, with gestures, and with face;
No more than mouth need move when words are said,
No more than hand to strike, or point ahead;
   Like slaves, limbs learn their place.

In triumph as in mutiny unmoved,
These make their public act their private good,
Their words in lounge or courtroom understood,
   But themselves never loved.

The eyes that will not look, the twitching cheek,
The hands that sketch what mouth would fear to own,
These only make us known, and we are known
   Only as we are weak:

By yielding mastery the will is freed,
For it is by surrender that we live,
And we are taken if we wish to give,
   Are needed if we need.

From *A Case of Samples* by Kingsley Amis. Harcourt, Brace and Company. Copyright 1956 by Kingsley Amis.

THE SOURCES OF THE PAST

by KINGSLEY AMIS

A broken flower-stem, a broken vase,
  A match-box torn in two and thrown
Among the lumps of glass:
  At the last meeting, these alone
Record its ruptures, point its violence,
  And, it seems, are ready to maintain
This charted look of permanence
  In the first moment's pain.

But now the door slams, the steps retreat;
  Into one softness night will blur
The diverse, the hard street;
  And memory will soon prefer

That polished set of symbols, glass and
  rose
  (By slight revision), to the real mess
Of stumbling, arguing, yells, blows
  Or tears: to real distress.

All fragments of the past, near and far,
  Come down to us framed in a calm
No contemplations jar;
  But they grub it up from lapse of time,
And, could we strip that firm order away,
  What crude agitation would be shown:
What aimless hauntings behind clay,
  What fevers behind stone?

A DREAM OF FAIR WOMEN

by KINGSLEY AMIS

The door still swinging to, and girls re-
  vive,
Aeronauts in the utmost altitudes
  Of boredom fainting, dive
Into the bright oxygen of my nod;
Angels as well, a squadron of draped
  nudes,
  They roar towards their god.

Militant all, they fight to take my hat,
No more as yet; the other men retire
  Insulted, gestured at;
Each girl presses on me her share of what
Makes up the barn-door target of desire;
  And I am a crack shot.

Speech fails them, amorous, but each one's
  look,

Endorsed in other ways, begs me to sign
  Her body's autograph-book;
"Me first, Kingsley; I'm cleverest," each
  declares,
But no gourmet races downstairs to dine,
  Nor will I race upstairs.

Feigning aplomb, perhaps for half an
  hour, .
I hover, and am shown by each princess
  The entrance to her tower,
Open, in that its tenant throws the key
At once to anyone, but not unless
  That anyone is me.

Now from the corridor their fathers cheer,
Their brothers, their young men; the
  cheers increase
  As soon as I appear;

The World, the Times

From each I win a handshake and sin-
  cere
Congratulations; from the chief of police
A nod, a wink, a leer.

This over, all delay is over too;
The first eight girls (the roster now
  agreed)
  Leap on me and undo . . .
But honesty impels me to confess
That this is "all a dream," which was, in-
  deed,
  Not difficult to guess.

But wait: not "just a dream," because,
  though good
And beautiful, it is also true, and hence
  Is rarely understood;

Who would choose any feasible ideal
In here and now's giant circumference
  If that small room were real?

Only the best; the others find, have found
Love's ordinary distances too great,
  And eager, stand their ground;
Map-drunk explorers, dry-land sailors,
  they
See no arrival that can compensate
  For boredom on the way.

And, seeming doctrinaire, but really weak,
Limelighted dolls guttering in their brain,
  They come with me, to seek
The halls of theoretical delight,
The women of that ever-fresh terrain,
  The night after tonight.

THE WORLD, THE TIMES

by DONALD HALL

The habit of these years is constant choice.
Each act, each moment, is political.
Enormous power responds to one man's
  voice.
The President and Cabinet are on call.
Great freedom walks in us, and we com-
  mand
The universe forever to expand.

The world, the times, the country, and the
  age
Maneuver toward eventuality.
We wait the coming; maybe in a rage
Great conquerors will come, our leaders
  be,
To take the generations into war
Until we men and women are no more;

Or maybe at some Easter we will find
A martyr who by absence wins the earth,
Who walked in life before us who were
  blind,
And whom we will await in second birth;
So live in holy darkness, and be sure
Our souls if not our bodies are secure.

However may the future be disguised,
I praise the moment, when no world is
  made.
Anarchy works to kill the civilized
And nothing will prevent a mortal raid
Except defense with violence again
Within the minds of many single men.

Now men are Persian in their ease, and
  fling

All difficulties out, for the freed man
Believes no good or ill in anything,
But loves his minute's pleasure, or what
can
So glorify his days that they will be
Productive of his own security.

There's no security except the grave;
There's much belief in what does not
exist.
All that is excellent is hard to save,
Since every man is partly anarchist.

We live by choice, and choose with every
act
That form or chaos move from mind to
fact.

I name an age of choice and discontent
Whose emblem is "the difficult to choose."
Each man is free to act, but his intent
Must circumscribe what he may not re-
fuse.
Each moment is political, and we
Are clothed in nothing but mortality.

LOVE CALLS US TO THE THINGS OF THIS WORLD

by RICHARD WILBUR

The eyes open to a cry of pulleys,
And spirited from sleep, the astounded soul
Hangs for a moment bodiless and simple
As false dawn.
          Outside the open window
The morning air is all awash with angels.

Some are in bed-sheets, some are in blouses,
Some are in smocks: but truly there they are.
Now they are rising together in calm swells
Of halcyon feeling, filling whatever they wear
With the deep joy of their impersonal breathing;

Now they are flying in place, conveying
The terrible speed of their omnipresence, moving
And staying like white water; and now of a sudden
They swoon down into so rapt a quiet
That nobody seems to be there.
          The soul shrinks

From all that it is about to remember
From the punctual rape of every blessèd day,
And cries,
        "Oh, let there be nothing on earth but laundry,

Nothing but rosy hands in the rising steam
And clear dances done in the sight of heaven."

Yet, as the sun acknowledges
With a warm look the world's hunks and colors,
The soul descends once more in bitter love
To accept the waking body, saying now
In a changed voice as the man yawns and rises,

"Bring them down from their ruddy gallows;
Let there be clean linen for the backs of thieves;
Let lovers go fresh and sweet to be undone,
And the heaviest nuns walk in a pure floating
Of dark habits,
                         keeping their difficult balance."

LOOKING INTO HISTORY

by RICHARD WILBUR

I. Five soldiers fixed by Mathew Brady's eye
   Stand in a land subdued beyond belief.
   Belief might lend them life again. I try
   Like orphaned Hamlet working up his grief

   To see my spellbound fathers in these men
   Who, breathless in their amber atmosphere,
   Show but the postures men affected then
   And the hermit faces of a finished year.

   The guns and gear and all are strange until
   Beyond the tents I glimpse a file of trees
   Verging a road that struggles up a hill.
   They're sycamores.

                         The long-abated breeze

   Flares in those boughs I know, and hauls the sound
   Of guns and a great forest in distress.
   Fathers, I know my cause, and we are bound
   Beyond that hill to fight at Wilderness.

II. But trick your eyes with Birnam Wood, or think
    How fire-cast shadows of the bankside trees

Rode on the back of Simois to sink
In the wide waters. Reflect how history's

Changes are like the sea's, which mauls and mulls
Its salvage of the world in shifty waves,
Shrouding in evergreen the oldest hulls
And yielding views of its confounded graves

To the new moon, the sun, or any eye
That in its shallow shoreward version sees
The pebbles charging with a deathless cry
And caragreen memorials of trees.

III. Now, old man of the sea,
      I start to understand:
      The will will find no stillness
      Back in a stilled land.

The dead give no command
And shall not find their voice
Till they be mustered by
Some present fatal choice.

Let me now rejoice
In all impostures, take
The shape of lion or leopard,
Boar, or watery snake,

Or like the comber break,
Yet in the end stand fast
And by some fervent fraud
Father the waiting past,

Resembling at the last
The self-established tree
That draws all waters toward
Its live formality.

RECORDINGS OF POEMS

A NUMBER of modern poets can be heard reading their own poems on records. Various companies and services supply these records, among them Columbia, Decca, Erpi Classroom Films, Inc., Harvard, HBC, HMV, Library of Congress, Linguaphone, Musicraft, The National Council of Teachers of English, Timely, Victor, and Caedmon.

Among the poets who have recorded their poems are:

Léonie Adams	Library of Congress
Conrad Aiken	Library of Congress
W. H. Auden	Linguaphone, NCTE, Columbia, Caedmon, Library of Congress
George Barker	Harvard
S. V. Benét	NCTE
John Berryman	Library of Congress
Elizabeth Bishop	Columbia
J. P. Bishop	NCTE
Richard Blackmur	Library of Congress
Louise Bogan	Library of Congress
John M. Brinnin	Library of Congress
R. P. T. Coffin	Linguaphone, NCTE
E. E. Cummings	HBC, NCTE, Columbia, Caedmon, Library of Congress
Walter de la Mare	HMV
Richard Eberhart	Harvard, Library of Congress
T. S. Eliot	Harvard, Columbia, Library of Congress
William Empson	Library of Congress
Paul Engle	Library of Congress
J. G. Fletcher	Harvard, Library of Congress
Robert Frost	Erpi, NCTE, Library of Congress
Horace Gregory	Library of Congress
Robert Hillyer	Harvard
John Holmes	Harvard
Randall Jarrell	Library of Congress
Robinson Jeffers	Harvard, Library of Congress
Vachel Lindsay	Linguaphone, NCTE
Robert Lowell	Library of Congress
Edwin Markham	Timely
Archibald MacLeish	Linguaphone, NCTE, Caedmon
Edna St. V. Millay	Victor
Marianne Moore	Columbia, NCTE, Library of Congress
Ogden Nash	Columbia
J. C. Ransom	Library of Congress

Recordings of Poems

Theodore Roethke	Library of Congress
Muriel Rukeyser	Library of Congress
Carl Sandburg	Decca, Musicraft
Delmore Schwartz	Library of Congress
Karl Shapiro	Library of Congress
Theodore Spencer	Library of Congress
Stephen Spender	Harvard, Library of Congress
Allen Tate	NCTE, Library of Congress
Dylan Thomas	Columbia, Caedmon
R. P. Warren	Library of Congress
W. C. Williams	Columbia, NCTE, Library of Congress
Yvor Winters	Library of Congress
Mark Van Doren	Library of Congress
Marya Zaturenska	Library of Congress

SOME BOOKS ON MODERN POETRY

THE reader who is interested in further study of modern poets and what their poems have meant to others may wish to consult some of the following volumes. The works listed here, only a few of those available, present varying points of view and assessments of modern poetry.

ARNHEIM and others: *Poets at Work* (1948)

BROOKS, CLEANTH: *Modern Poetry and the Tradition* (1939), *The Well Wrought Urn* (1947)

DAICHES, DAVID: *Poetry and the Modern World* (1940)

DREW AND SWEENEY: *Directions in Modern Poetry* (1940)

DURRELL, LAWRENCE: *A Key to Modern British Poetry* (1952)

FRANKENBERG, LLOYD: *Pleasure Dome: On Reading Modern Poetry* (1949)

GREGORY AND ZATURENSKA: *History of Modern American Poetry* (1946)

HOUSMAN, A. E.: *The Name and Nature of Poetry* (1933)

JARRELL, RANDALL: *Poetry and the Age* (1953)

LEAVIS, F. R.: *New Bearings in English Poetry* (1932)

LEWIS, C. DAY: *A Hope for Poetry* (1935), *The Poetic Image* (1947)

LOWES, J. L.: *Convention and Revolt in Poetry* (1919)

MACNEICE, LOUIS: *Modern Poetry* (1938)

RAYMOND, MARCEL: *From Baudelaire to Surrealism* (1950)

SAVAGE, D. S.: *The Personal Principle: Studies in Modern Poetry* (1944)

SCARFE, FRANCIS: *Auden and After* (1942)

SHAPIRO, KARL: *Essay on Rime* (1945)

SMITH, CHARD P.: *Pattern and Variation in Poetry* (1932)

SPENDER, STEPHEN: *The Destructive Element* (1934), *The Creative Element* (1954)

STAUFFER, DONALD A.: *The Nature of Poetry* (1946)

TATE, ALLEN: *Reactionary Essays on Poetry* (1938)

TINDALL, W. Y.: *Forces in Modern British Literature* (1947)

WAGGONER, H. H.: *The Heel of Elohim* (1950)

WELLS, HENRY: *New Poets from Old* (1940)

WILSON, EDMUND: *Axel's Castle* (1931)

WINTERS, YVOR: *In Defense of Reason* (1947)

BIOGRAPHICAL NOTES

KINGSLEY AMIS (1922-), whose poems *A Frame of Mind* appeared in 1953, is teaching at the University of Swansea, Swansea, Wales. His novel *Lucky Jim*, 1956, has aroused great interest in England.

MATTHEW ARNOLD (1822-1888) was a graduate of Balliol College, Oxford, winning the Newdigate prize in poetry in 1843. He was inspector of schools from 1851 to 1886 and professor of poetry in Oxford from 1857 to 1867. He lectured widely and was in America in 1883-1884 and 1886. His critical works include two series of *Essays in Criticism*, 1865, 1888, *Culture and Anarchy*, 1869, and *Literature and Dogma*, 1873; his poems were collected in 1890.

W. H. AUDEN (1907-) was born at York, England, and educated at Christ Church College, Oxford. He taught for a time. In 1937 he served as an ambulance driver for the Loyalist forces in the Spanish Civil War. In 1939 he came to the United States and took out citizenship papers. He has taught at the New School for Social Research, the University of Michigan, and Swarthmore. His *Collected Poems* appeared in 1945. Later volumes are *The Age of Anxiety*, 1947, *Nones*, 1951, and *The Shield of Achilles*, 1955.

ROBERT CONQUEST (1917-) has published in English literary journals, and has edited an anthology of new British poets. His first volume of *Poems* appeared in 1955.

E. E. CUMMINGS (1894-) was born in Cambridge, Massachusetts, and graduated from Harvard in 1915. He received his M.A. the following year. He was a volunteer ambulance driver in France before the entry of the United States into World War I. After the war he lived in Paris for a time, then returned to New York. He made a trip to Russia in 1930. His novel, *The Enormous Room*, was published in 1922. His poetry includes *Collected Poems*, 1938, *Fifty Poems*, 1940, *1 X 1*, 1934, and *XAIPE: seventy-one poems*, 1950.

ROBERT DAY (1900-) was born in California and studied at the Otis Art Institute. He began work as a cartoonist for the Los Angeles *Times* and was later in the art departments of the Los Angeles *Examiner* and the New York *Herald Tribune*. In addition to drawings for advertisements, he has published *All Out for the Sack Race!* and illustrated *We Shook the Family Tree*. He is a frequent contributor to *The New Yorker* and *The Saturday Evening Post*.

ABNER DEAN (1910-) was born in New York. After graduating from Dartmouth in 1931, he experimented with various art forms, published for some years cartoons and covers for *The New Yorker*. His work gained a wider notice with the publication of seven of his drawings in *Life* magazine and the consequent recognition given to his collections, *It's a long way to Heaven*, 1945, and *What am I doing here?*, 1947.

EMILY DICKINSON (1830-1886) was born in Amherst, Mass., into the quiet life and religious atmosphere of a very conservative town. She studied at the Academy founded by her grandfather, and for one year at the Mount Holyoke Female Seminary. When she was twenty-three years old, she journeyed to Washington to visit her father who was serving in Congress. After 1856 she virtually isolated herself in the family home for the rest of her life, and there wrote the poems which were neither known nor published until after her death. There has been much speculation over the reasons for this self-imposed isolation. Her 1862 letter to T. W. Higginson may provide a clue.

When a little girl, I had a friend who taught me Immortality; but venturing too near, himself, he never returned. Soon after, my tutor died, and for several years my lexicon was my only companion. Then I found one more, but he was not contented I be his scholar, so he left the land.

The majority of her poems are found in *Poems,* 1890, Second Series, 1891, Third Series, 1896, *Poems,* 1930, *Bolts of Melody,* 1945.

T. S. ELIOT (1888-   ) was born in St. Louis, Missouri. He graduated with an M.A. in 1910 from Harvard, where his classmates included Heywood Broun, John Reed, Walter Lippmann and Stuart Chase. He has lived in England since 1915, and became a British subject in 1927. In 1928 he announced that he was "an Anglo-Catholic in religion, a classicist in literature, and a royalist in politics." His poetic works include *Collected Poems: 1909-1935, Four Quartets,* 1943, and the poetic plays, *Murder in the Cathedral,* 1935, *The Family Reunion,* 1939, *The Cocktail Party,* 1950 and *The Confidential Clerk,* 1954. Among his collections of essays are *Selected Essays: 1917-1932, Essays Ancient and Modern,* 1936, *The Idea of a Christian Society,* 1940, and *Notes towards the Definition of Culture,* 1949.

RALPH WALDO EMERSON (1803-1882) was born in Boston and educated at Harvard. Entering the ministry, he became pastor of the Second (Unitarian) Church of Boston, but personal and theological difficulties caused him to leave the ministry in 1832. Travel in America and Europe, where he met Coleridge, Wordsworth, Carlyle, and lecturing and writing occupied his later life. Edwin Arlington Robinson regarded Emerson as America's greatest 19th Century poet, but Emerson was modest about his poetry, writing, "I feel it a hardship that—with something of a lover's passion for what is to me the most precious thing in life, poetry —I have no gift of fluency in it, only a rude

and stammering utterance." Among his important works are *Nature,* 1836, *Essays,* First Series, 1841, *Poems,* 1847, *The Conduct of Life,* 1860, and *Society and Solitude,* 1870.

KENNETH FEARING (1902-   ) was born in Oak Park, Illinois. He attended the University of Illinois, but transferred to and graduated from the University of Wisconsin in 1924. He worked at selling, free-lance writing, journalism, and for a time taught poetry at the League of American Writers in New York. He has said that poetry "must be exciting; otherwise it is valueless. . . . Besides being exciting, I think that poetry necessarily must be understandable." Among his books are *Collected Poems,* 1940, and *Afternoon of a Pawnbroker and Other Poems,* 1943.

IAIN FLETCHER (1920-   ) is a member of the English Department at the University of Reading, England. His poems have appeared in *Poetry, London.*

ROBERT FROST (1875-   ) was born in San Francisco. After the death of his father in 1885, his mother took her children to Lawrence, Massachusetts. Eventually, he attended Dartmouth for a few months, and Harvard for two years, but left college to teach and farm. He moved to England in 1912, where his first two books of poems were published—his first major recognition. In 1915 he returned to the United States. He has lectured and taught in various colleges, principally at Amherst. His work includes *Collected Poems,* 1939, *A Witness Tree,* 1942, *A Masque of Reason,* 1945, *A Masque of Mercy,* 1947, and *Steeple Bush,* 1947.

DONALD HALL (1928-   ), after study and travel abroad, was awarded a Fellowship at Harvard. His volume *Exiles and Marriages* was the Lamont Poetry Selection for 1955. He is at present the Poetry Editor of *The Paris Review.*

THOMAS HARDY (1840-1928) was born in Dorsetshire. After brief schooling he served as an architect's apprentice for several years. He became increasingly interested in creative writing, particularly in poetry but "necessity" turned him to the writing of novels. The first of his many novels appeared in 1871. His brilliant career as novelist was brought to a close by the critical attack on *Tess of the D'Urbervilles* and *Jude the Obscure*. "Cured of all interest in novel-writing," as he said, at the age of 58 he returned to poetry. He gradually won over an at first apathetic public, and his *Collected Poems* in 1919 showed his power as a poet. He continued to write until his death at the age of 88. In addition to his novels, short stories, and poems, he completed in 1908 an epic drama of the Napoleonic Wars, *The Dynasts*.

MARSDEN HARTLEY (1877-1943), painter and poet, was born in Lewiston, Maine, and spent his early years in Cleveland, Ohio. After study at the National Academy in New York and in Europe, he settled in New York City to paint the strongly colored, often symbolic and almost abstract landscapes and figures now in many American collections and museums. His first work, shown by Alfred Stieglitz in 1908, caused some critical controversy, but he continued to hold one-man exhibits for 30 years. In 1930 he won a Guggenheim Fellowship for study in Mexico. His poems and reproductions of some of his paintings are in *Selected Poems*, 1945.

GEOFFREY HILL (1932-   ) is a member of the English Department at the University of Leeds, England. His first volume of poems is to be published in London in 1958.

EDWARD HOPPER (1882-   ), American artist, has won many prizes and medals for his prints and paintings. He was born in Nyack, New York, and after attending public and private schools he studied at the New York School of Art under Chase and

Henri. His works hang in a number of American museums, libraries, and private collections, and he is also a contributor to magazines.

A. E. HOUSMAN (1859-1936) was born in Worcestershire and attended St. John's College, Oxford. He failed his fourth-year honors examinations, but returned for one term of study to pass the degree. From 1882 to 1892 he was a clerk in the Government Patent Office in London. He continued his classical studies at night and won a reputation as a brilliant classical scholar. In 1892 he was appointed Professor of Latin in University College, London, and in 1911 received the same appointment in Trinity College, Cambridge, a position which he held until his death. He once said he was "not a pessimist but a pejorist." *A Shropshire Lad* was published in 1896, *Last Poems* in 1922. *More Poems*, a posthumous collection, appeared in 1936. His essay, *The Name and Nature of Poetry*, was printed in 1933.

ROBINSON JEFFERS (1887-   ) was born in Pittsburgh. He lived in Europe from 1899 until 1902. In 1905 he received his A.B. from Occidental College. He did some graduate work in forestry and medicine. In 1912 a legacy made him independent, and two years later he settled permanently at Carmel, California, where he built his famous stone tower. Among his books are *Selected Poetry*, 1938, *Be Angry at the Sun*, 1941, *Medea* (an adaptation of the Greek tragedy), 1946, and *The Double Axe*, 1948.

LUIGI LUCIONI (1900-   ) was born in Italy and came to the United States in 1911. He studied at the Cooper Union Art School (1916-1920) and the National Academy of Design (1920-1925). His work is represented by many paintings and etchings in American galleries and collections. He won the Tiffany medal in 1928, the first popular prize at the Carnegie International Exhibition in 1939 and in the same year the first popular prize at the Biennial Exhibition in Washington, D. C.

ARCHIBALD MacLEISH (1892-   ) was born in Glencoe, Illinois. He received his B.A. from Yale in 1915, and his LL.B. from Harvard in 1919. He enlisted in the Field Artillery in 1917 and was discharged as a captain. From 1923 to 1928 he traveled abroad. On his return he worked on *Fortune* magazine. In 1939 he was named Librarian of Congress, and in 1941 was appointed Director of Office of Facts and Figures (which later became the Office of War Information under Elmer Davis). For a while he served as Under-Secretary of State. Among his books are *Selected Poems: 1924-1933, Public Speech,* 1936, *America Was Promises,* 1939, the two radio plays, *The Fall of the City,* 1937, and *Air Raid,* 1938, and his essays, *The Irresponsibles,* 1940, *The American Cause,* 1941, and *A Time to Speak,* 1941. Since 1949 he has been Boylston Professor at Harvard University, and has contributed to many magazines. *Actfive and Other Poems* was published in 1948, and *Collected Poems* in 1952.

MARY PETTY lives in New York City and is married to Alan Dunn, the artist. In addition to drawing cartoons and covers for *The New Yorker,* she has illustrated *Goodbye, Mr. Chippendale* by T. H. Robsjohn-Gibbings and a new edition of Dickens' *Martin Chuzzlewit.* Of the people in her drawings she has said, "I'm afraid I am like the people I draw, of whom Harold Ross is reported to have once said, 'They look like something that lives under a rock.'"

EDWIN ARLINGTON ROBINSON (1869-1935) was born in Head Tide, Maine. He spent two years at Harvard, then went to New York, where he worked on new subway construction, lived very frugally and continued his writing. In 1905 President Theodore Roosevelt, who had read and been impressed by his poems, had him appointed to the New York Customs House. After 1911

Robinson spent his summers at the Mac-Dowell Colony in Peterboro, New Hampshire, and his winters in New York. His *Collected Poems* was printed in 1937.

CARL SANDBURG (1878-   ) was born in Galesburg, Illinois. He left school at thirteen and worked at miscellaneous jobs for several years. During the Spanish-American War he enlisted and served in Puerto Rico for eight months. After his discharge he worked his way at Lombard College but did not graduate. He then engaged in newspaper work, and for a time was secretary to the Socialist mayor of Milwaukee. After 1914, his poetry began to win him wide recognition. His poetry includes *Selected Poems,* 1926, *The People, Yes,* 1936, and *Home Front Memo,* 1943. He has also published a biography: *Abraham Lincoln, the Prairie Years,* 1926, and *Abraham Lincoln, the War Years,* 1939.

E. J. SCOVELL (1907-   ) has published her poems in *The River Steamer,* 1956.

STEPHEN SPENDER (1909-   ) was born in London. He attended University College, Oxford, where he met and worked with W. H. Auden and Louis MacNeice. In 1937 he went to Spain to attend the International Writers Congress, and remained there for several months during the Civil War. His sympathies were with the Loyalists. During World War II he was in or near London, and served as a fireman through the blitz. His work includes *Poems,* 1933, *The Still Centre,* 1939, *Ruins and Visions,* 1942, *Poems of Dedication,* 1947, *The Edge of Being,* 1949, and the prose volumes, *The Destructive Element,* 1934, *European Witness,* 1946, and an autobiography, *World within World,* 1951.

DYLAN THOMAS (1914-1953) was born in Wales. After an early career in journalism and film scripting, he published *18 Poems* in 1934, saying that the poems were, "the record of my individual struggle from darkness towards some measure of light . . . My poetry is or should be useful to others for its individual recording of that same struggle with which they are necessarily acquainted." During the War he worked for the BBC. In 1950-52 he traveled in the United States reading his poems at many colleges. His important collections are *The World I Breathe*, 1939, *Selected Writings*, 1946, *In Country Sleep*, 1952, and *Collected Poems*, 1953.

JAMES THURBER (1894-   ) was born in Columbus, Ohio, and educated at Ohio State University. For a time he was a reporter and writer on the Paris edition of the Chicago *Tribune*. He returned to New York in 1926, and began contributing humorous sketches, stories and drawings to *The New Yorker*. His books include *The Owl in the Attic and Other Perplexities*, 1931, *My Life and Hard Times*, 1933, *My World—and Welcome to It*, 1942, *The Thurber Carnival*, 1945, and *The Thurber Album*, 1952.

WALT WHITMAN (1819-1892), was born on Long Island. Brief schooling followed the family's removal to Brooklyn, and young Whitman went to work as a "printer's devil" and typesetter. Years of hack-work as a printer-journalist led to his editorship of the *Brooklyn Eagle*. After two years he left, and there followed years of unsuccessful journalism, of carpentry with his father, of lecturing. In 1855 his publication of *Leaves of Grass* brought high praise from Emerson, but abuse and incomprehension from others. He continued with his poetry, and the 3d Edition of *Leaves of Grass* in 1860 contained 157 poems. During the Civil War he worked as a volunteer nurse in army hospitals, and for some years after the War as a government clerk. In 1873 he suffered a paralytic stroke which forced him to leave Washington. He settled in Camden, N. J., where he remained, a semi-invalid, for the rest of his life. In 1891 he was able to attend a dinner where he received the congratulations of some of the most distinguished Americans and Englishmen for his writing. His other works were *Drum Taps*, 1865, *Democratic Vistas*, 1871.

RICHARD WILBUR (1921-   ), after study at Amherst and Harvard, taught at Harvard and at Wellesley. His volume *Things of This World* won the National Book Award for poetry in 1956.

WILLIAM BUTLER YEATS (1865-1939) was born in Dublin. He first studied art, then turned to writing. He worked to encourage an Irish literary renaissance. For four years he was a Senator of the Irish Free State. He was awarded the Nobel Prize in 1923. His books include *Collected Poems*, 1933, *Collected Plays*, 1934, and *Last Poems and Plays*, 1940.

INDEX OF AUTHORS, TITLES,
AND FIRST LINES

Index of Authors, Titles, and First Lines